Religious Studies (A2 Ethics)

Revision Guide

Peter Baron

2011-2012 Edition

Published by Inducit Learning Ltd trading as pushmepress.com,

Pawlett House ,West Street, Somerton,

Somerset TA11 7PS, United Kingdom

www.pushmepress.com

First published in 2011

ISBN: 978-1-4716-3632-5

All rights reserved. No part of this publication may be reproduced, stored in a retrieval system, or in any form or by any means, without the prior permission in writing of the publisher, nor otherwise circulated in any form of binding or cover other than that in which it is published and without a similar condition including this condition bring imposed on the subsequent publisher.

© Inducit Learning Ltd

Cartoons used with permission © Becky Dyer

All images © their respective owners

Contents

Introduction to ethics 5
Meta-Ethics 9
Free will and Determinism 25
Behaviourism 39
Conscience 47
Virtue Ethics 63
Business Ethics 75
Environmental Ethics 85
Sexual Ethics 105
Exam Rescue Remedy 121
Postscript 123

'The unexamined life is not worth living' Socrates

Introduction to ethics

At AS level we introduced **DEONTOLOGICAL** and **TELEOLOGICAL** ethics and asked the question: to what extent is ethics **ABSOLUTE** or **RELATIVE**? We then applied the ethical theories to abortion, euthanasia, genetic engineering and war and peace.

At A2 the theories are now retained and a number of new issues considered, notably the **FREE WILL** debate and theories of **CONSCIENCE**. To deontology and teleology we add **ARETAIC** (virtue) ethics – the ethics of character and **META-ETHICS**, the study of ethical meaning.

APPLIED ISSUES AT A2

1. **ENVIRONMENTAL ETHICS**
2. **BUSINESS ETHICS**
3. **SEXUAL ETHICS** (homosexuality, sex before marriage, adultery and contraception)

KEY TERMS

- Meta-ethics concerns the nature and meaning of the words good and right. A key question in meta-ethics is: "Is goodness **OBJECTIVE** (linked to moral facts in the world) or **SUBJECTIVE** (up to me)?"

- Virtue ethics studies virtues and vices as **CHARACTER** traits or **HABITS**. Virtue ethics asks: "What character traits do I need to practise to build the excellent life?"

- Determinists see every event, including human choice, as having an antecedent **CAUSE**. The question arises: "Where does this leave moral **RESPONSIBILITY** and free will?"

- Conscience may come from **GOD**, our **UPBRINGING** or a process of **REASON**. "Where does conscience come from and how does it operate?" **PSYCHOLOGY** merges with philosophy here.

- Intrinsic theories of value see something as good-in-itself. Does the environment have intrinsic value? Which part of it?

- Instrumental theories of value see goodness relative to some end, such as human happiness. But in the debates within ethics, what do **DEONTOLOGISTS** like Kant or **TELEOLOGISTS** like Joseph Fletcher have to say about sexual ethics?

- Globalisation implies an increasingly integrated global economy and culture, where free trade, free flow of capital and free allocation of resources enables **MULTINATIONAL** companies to pursue the end of least cost labour and raw materials. A key question arises: "Are their ends and practices ethical?"

THE ETHICS TOOLKIT

The study of ethical theories so far has equipped us with a toolkit which we can use to assess any ethical issue. In this toolkit we derive insights from different theories.

KANT has given us the **PRINCIPLE OF UNIVERSALISABILITY**, a method of reasoning implying **CONSISTENCY** and a neutral point of view, and **PERSONAL AUTONOMY**, that places human choice and reason as a central ethical concern.

AQUINAS has given us the **PRINCIPLE OF NATURAL RATIONAL PURPOSE:** the idea of an order of being which is appropriate to our unique rational natures. The ultimate **TELOS** is **EUDAIMONIA** – well-being or personal and social flourishing.

UTILITARIANS have given us the **LEAST HARM PRINCIPLE**: the idea that we should always assess consequences in the light of an empirical calculation of the balance of happiness over misery, pleasure over pain or **WELFARE** over harm. In Economics we talk of **COST/ BENEFIT** analysis.

RELATIVISTS encourage us to consider the **PRINCIPLE OF CULTURAL DIVERSITY** and to be humble in the face of claims that our own culture is objectively superior. All theories are to some extent children of their times.

It is important to note that our theories overlap to some extent and may not be as opposed as we sometimes think. For example, all of them discuss and claim for themselves the **GOLDEN RULE** "Do to others as you would have them do to you", Matthew 7:18 (is this therefore a good example of a universal ethical absolute?).

All appeal to **VIRTUE** or character traits (**MILL** appeals to sympathy, **KANT** to dutifulness, **FLETCHER** to love, **AQUINAS** to practical wisdom and the Christian virtues of I Corinthians 13, faith, hope and love).

All theories have a **TELEOLOGICAL** aspect. Kant for example considers consequences in so far as he asks us to universalise the consequences of everyone doing what I do. He also envisages a goal, the **SUMMUM BONUM** which is similar in some ways to Aristotle's **EUDAIMONIA**. Moreover, Aquinas' **NATURAL LAW** is best described as "a deontological theory arising out of a Greek teleological worldview" where the good is defined by the rational ends (**TELOS**).

And our third deontological theory – **DIVINE COMMAND** whilst revering the rules of God, also sees the ultimate end to be like Christ, fulfilling our true humanity which is perfected in him, in the afterlife and also (crucially) the present age which is a society called the **KINGDOM OF GOD** – one family where love and justice are supreme.

Interestingly, **R.M.HARE** who we meet in the **META-ETHICS** section with his theory of **PRESCRIPTIVISM** is a Kantian preference utilitarian (and former tutor of Peter Singer).

Meta-Ethics

META-ETHICS means "beyond ethics" (metaphysics - beyond physics). Rather than asking how we derive moral principles like "do not kill", meta-ethics asks us to consider what moral statements mean. Here are some of the key issues:

1. Is there an objective principle we can appeal to resolve moral disputes? Or are we inevitably in a world of **RELATIVISM** and **SUBJECTIVISM** where such questions are "up to me"?

2. When I say "stealing is wrong" am I describing some **FACTS** about the world which we can look at, examine, appeal to, or am I only stating an opinion or expressing a feeling?

3. Is moral **LANGUAGE** a special type of language where words like "good" and "ought" mean something quite specific and different from other uses of, for example, "good"? Is the meaning of good in the sentence "that's a good painting" different from the moral use "good boy!"?

KEY TERMS

- **Analytic** - true by definition "all bachelors are unmarried".

- **Synthetic** - true by observation "John is a bachelor".

- **A priori** - before experience

- **A posteriori** - after experience

- **Cognitivism** - moral facts can be known objectively

- **Naturalism** - moral goodness is a feature of the natural world, and so an a posteriori fact

- **Naturalistic fallacy** - you cannot move without supplying a missing **PREMISE** from a descriptive statement such as "kindness causes pleasure" to a moral statement "kindness is good".

Note: Hume was himself a naturalist arguing that morality derives from the natural feeling of sympathy. He never said "you cannot move from an ought to an is", but only that if we do so, we must provide a missing premise with a value-statement in it, such as "pleasure is good as it leads to a happy life".

COGNITIVE or NON-COGNITIVE

COGNITIVISTS believe goodness can be known as an **OBJECTIVE** feature of the world - where "objective" means "out there where it can be analysed, measured, and assessed".

Something about our reason allows us to do this either by making some measurement (for example of happiness as the utilitarians do) or working out a principle **A PRIORI**, before experience, as Kant argues we do in deriving the **CATEGORICAL IMPERATIVE**.

NON-COGNITIVISTS argue there is no objective, factual basis for morality - it is subjective and up to me to determine.

The **NATURALISTS** argue we can resolve this issue empirically (**A POSTERIORI** - from experience) by looking at some observable feature of an action - a fact such as "it causes pain" (a utilitarian concern) or "it fulfils the natural rational purpose of human beings" (the **EUDAIMONIA** of virtue ethics).

NON-NATURALISTS argue either that the truth is a priori (Kant for example) or that there are simply no facts which we can identify as moral facts – so that making a moral statement adds nothing to what we already know from a factual basis. This form of non-naturalism is called **EMOTIVISM**.

THE NATURALISTIC FALLACY

Starting with David Hume philosophers like **GE MOORE** have argued that when we move from a description about the real world to a moral statement we make a leap from a naturalistic statement to a **PRESCRIPTIVE** statement (one with ought in it). This prescription is doing something different. What we often fail to do is explain the missing link between a description and a prescription - and this leap from is to ought is what is known as the naturalistic fallacy. A.N. Prior explains the fallacy:

> "The assumption that because some quality or combination of qualities invariably and necessarily accompanies the quality of goodness, or is invariably and necessarily accompanied by it, or both, this quality or combination of qualities is identical with goodness. If, for example, it is believed that whatever is pleasant is and must be good, or that whatever is good is and must be pleasant, or both, it is committing the naturalistic fallacy to infer from this that goodness and pleasantness are one and the same quality. The naturalistic fallacy is the assumption that because the words 'good' and, say, 'pleasant' necessarily describe the same objects, they must attribute the same quality to them". (1949)

MOORE argued that goodness cannot be a **COMPLEX** analysable property of an action. For example a horse can be broken down into animal, mammal, four legs, hairy tail – a **COMPLEX** idea. Because goodness isn't a complex idea, it must be either a **SIMPLE**, indefinable quality or it doesn't refer to anything at all. Since ethics isn't an **ILLUSION**, goodness must consist in a simple **INDEFINABLE QUALITY**, like the colour yellow.

THE OPEN QUESTION

Moore pointed out that the naturalistic fallacy, of implying that goodness was identical to some specific property such as pleasure, is susceptible to the **OPEN QUESTION** attack. Suppose I say "this ice cream causes me so much pleasure" and then say "ice cream is good!" The open question attack suggests I can always ask the question "it produces pleasure, but nonetheless, is it morally **GOOD**?"

If I can answer "no" to this point then I have proved that goodness is something independent of pleasure.

MOORE's INTUITIONISM

Moore was a non-naturalist **COGNITIVIST** because he believed that goodness could not be defined by its natural properties, but that we know what we mean by good by a special intuition or perception (so **COGNITIVIST**, as goodness can be known as a shared experience).

Moore argues goodness is an **INDEFINABLE PROPERTY** of an action just as the colour yellow is a non-definable property of a lemon - we know what it is and that's the end of it. We can try and reduce yellowness to light waves but that doesn't precisely tell us what yellow is - yellow just is yellow, we know this by intuition. Notice this is a version of non-naturalism as goodness cannot be established as a fact of sense experience, but as a **NON-NATURALISTIC** perception.

EVALUATION OF INTUITIONISM

1. Moral intuitions are said to be like the **ANALYTIC** truths of Mathematics. But moral statements are more than just "true by definition". "Thus the intuitionists lost the one useful analogy to support the existence of a body of truths known by reason alone". Peter Singer

2. Intuitionists **CAN'T AGREE** what these moral goods are. So how can they be **SELF-EVIDENT**?

3. If intuitions are actually **CULTURAL CONSTRUCTS** as Freud suggests, then they cannot be **SELF-EVIDENT**.

4. Moore is arguing that moral truths are similar to **PLATO**'s ideal forms. John Maynard **KEYNES** once commented that "Moore could not distinguish love, and beauty and truth from the furniture" so enraptured was he by his idealised world of the forms.

5. Moore confuses a complex thing (colour) for a simple thing (yellow). Goodness is in fact a **COMPLEX** idea, like **COLOUR** because it includes within it a whole class of principles we might describe as good (like colour includes, red, yellow, green, blue).

Moore has confused a general category (colour, goodness) for a specific quality of that category (yellowness, generosity).

UTILITARIAN NATURALISM

Utilitarians are **NATURALISTS** because they argue that goodness is an observable feature of the natural world - part of our **A POSTERIORI** experience of pleasure and pain. So to work out what is good, we need to project into the future and balance the likely pain and pleasure of our choice. That which maximises happiness and minimises pain is good, and actions that do the opposite are bad.

Utilitarians quite openly commit the **NATURALISTIC FALLACY** arguing that it is obviously good to pursue happiness because that as a matter of fact is the goal that all humans are pursuing. They give a **TELEOLOGICAL** justification for goodness, just as virtue ethicists follow Aristotle in linking goodness to **HUMAN FLOURISHING**.

The philosopher **JOHN SEARLE** gives us another naturalist way out of the supposed fallacy. If I promise to pay you £500 then I am doing two things - I am agreeing to play the promising game which involves **OBLIGATION** to pay your money back, and I am accepting that part of the rules of the game, fixed by society, is that I only can break this promise if a large, overriding reason appears for doing so (for example, the money is stolen from me and I am bankrupt, so can't pay it back).

So the making of a promise is a **FACT** but because of the logical feature of promising - that I agree it creates obligations for me - this allows us to move to a value statement "you ought to keep your promise".

AYER's EMOTIVISM (expressivism)

A.J. Ayer (1910-1989) formed part of a school of linguistic philosophy called **LOGICAL POSITIVISM** which had at its heart the **VERIFICATION PRINCIPLE**. Truth claims had to be verified true or false by sense-experience. His theory is a theory of **NON-COGNITIVISM** as he argues moral statements add no facts – just opinions which cannot be established true or false empirically. So moral truth cannot be **KNOWN**.

> "The fundamental ethical concepts are unanalysable inasmuch as there is no criterion by which to judge the validity of the judgements. They are mere pseudo-concepts. The presence of an ethical symbol adds nothing to its factual content. Thus if I say to someone 'You acted wrongly in stealing the money,' I am not stating anything more than if I had simply stated 'you stole the money'". Language, Truth and Logic 1971

This approach to moral language was a development of **HUME's FORK** - an argument about language developed by David Hume. Hume argued that statements about the real world were of two sorts - they were either analytic or synthetic: either **LOGICAL TRUTHS** or **STATEMENTS OF FACT**.

An analytic statement is true by definition (2+2=4), a synthetic statement true by experience. So "all bachelors are unmarried" is true by definition, whereas "John is a bachelor" is true by experience (John might be married so that would make the statement **EMPIRICALLY** false). As moral statements are neither analytic (they'd have nothing useful to say about the **REAL** world if they were) or synthetic (not **VERIFIABLE**) they are logically and empirically meaningless.

Ayer put the same point another way.

> "The presence of an ethical symbol in a proposition adds nothing to its factual content". (1971:142).

Ayer believed that problems arose when the **NATURALISTS**, such as the **UTILITARIANS** claimed an empirical basis for goodness in the balance of pleasure over pain. What happens when one person's pleasure is another person's pain? Consider that someone steals your wallet. To you, stealing is wrong because it causes you pain. To the thief, stealing is good, because it gives her money to buy food, and she's starving. Stealing appears to be **BOTH** right and wrong at the same time.

This contradictory result indicates there can be no **FACT** of morality – just an **OPINION**.

> "It is not self-contradictory to say some pleasant things are not good, or that some bad things are desired". (1971:139)

Ayer means by this that if I say "you were wrong to steal" there is no additional **FACT** introduced by the word "wrong" - only an **EXPRESSION** of a feeling of disapproval. Note he argues the word **GOOD** is not describing a feeling but, in is own words "**EVINCING**" a feeling - like letting out a squeal if you hit your thumb.

> "Stealing money is wrong expresses no proposition which can be either true or false. It's as if I had written "stealing money!!!" where the exclamation marks show a special sort of moral disapproval". A.J. Ayer

EVALUATION OF AYER

1. Ayer's view seems to be a radical **SUBJECTIVISM** suggesting morality is just "up to me". It is a form of **RELATIVISM** that makes moral debate impossible.

2. Ayer's view is based on a **FALLACY**. Ludwig Wittgenstein demonstrated that language is part of a game we play with shared rules. **MORAL** language is neither analytic nor synthetic but rather, **PRESCRIPTIVE**. Ayer has committed a fallacy like saying "the world is either square or flat". It's neither.

3. According to Alasdair MacIntyre in After Virtue, emotivism obliterates the distinction between manipulative and non-manipulative behaviour. There is no longer such an idea as a **VALID REASON**. Moral discourse is simply about manipulating you to my point of view.

MORAL PROGRESS

C.L. STEVENSON's EMOTIVISM (interest theory)

Stevenson argued that three criteria must be fulfilled when we use the word "good":

1. We must be able to agree that the action is good.

2. The action must have a **MAGNETISM** - we must want to do it, and feel an **INTEREST** in its being done.

3. The action cannot be verified empirically by appeal to facts.

So moral language has an **EMOTIVE** meaning and a **PERSUASIVE** meaning – we are encouraging others to share our attitude. This is why we bother to **ARGUE** about ethics, whereas on questions of taste we "agree to differ".

> "Good has an emotive meaning...when a person morally approves of something, he experiences a rich feeling of security when it prospers and is indignant or shocked when it doesn't". CL Stevenson.

R.M.HARE's PRESCRIPTIVISM

R.M. Hare (1919-2002) argued that moral judgements have an **EMOTIVE** and a **PRESCRIPTIVE** meaning.

Prescriptions are forms of **IMPERATIVE**: "you oughtn't steal" is equivalent to saying "**DON'T STEAL!**".

Hare agrees that you cannot derive a **PRESCRIPTION** such as "run!" from a description "there's a bull over there!" as there is a **SUBJECTIVE** element (I may choose to walk calmly or stand and wave my red rag). I am free to judge, hence the title of his book **FREEDOM** and **REASON**.

Hare follows **KANT** (even though Hare is a preference utilitarian) in arguing that **REASONABLENESS** lies in the **UNIVERSALISABILITY** of moral statements. Anyone who uses terms like "right" and "ought" are **LOGICALLY COMMITTED** to the idea that any action in relevantly similar circumstances is also wrong (see Kant's first formula of the **CATEGORICAL IMPERATIVE**).

So if Nazis say "Jews must be killed", they must also judge that if, say it turns out that they are of Jewish origin then they too must be killed. Only a **FANATIC** would say this.

Hare argues for the importance of **MORAL PRINCIPLE**S rather than **RULES**. It is like learning to drive a car:

> "The good driver is one whose actions are so exactly governed by principles which have become a habit with him, that he normally does not have to think what to do. But all road conditions are various, and therefore it is unwise to let all one's driving become a matter of habit". Language of Morals page 63

EVALUATION OF PRESCRIPTIVISM

1. Hare is still denying there are **OBJECTIVE** moral truths. We are free to choose our own principles and determine our actions according to our desires and preferences – there is no objective right and wrong independent of our choosing, but then having chosen, we must be able to universalise it. As a **NON-NATURALIST** he avoids reference to any final **TELOS** such as human flourishing.

2. Philippa **FOOT** criticised Hare in her lecture in 1958 ("Moral Beliefs") for allowing terribly immoral acts (and people) to be called "moral" simply because they are **CONSISTENT**. We cannot avoid approving the statement "If I was a Jew, I would want to be dead too". Prescriptivism cannot help justifying **FANATICISM**.

3. In his later book **MORAL THINKING** Hare brings together **PRESCRIPTIVISM** and his version of **PREFERENCE UTILITARIANISM**. To prescribe a moral action is to universalise that action – in universalising "I must take into account all the ideals and preferences held by all those who will be affected and I cannot give any weight to my own ideals. The ultimate effect of this application of universalisability is that a moral judgement must ultimately be based on the maximum possible satisfaction of the preferences of all those affected by it".

4. Hare's pupil **PETER SINGER** builds on this idea to give prescriptivism an **OBJECTIVE** basis in his own version of preference utilitarianism. We are asked to universalise from a neutral, universal viewpoint.

So in the end prescriptivism escapes the charge of being another form of radical subjectivism.

THE LEGACY OF DAVID HUME

David Hume argued that morality was a matter of acting on desires and feelings. Moral reasoning really reduces to the question "what do I want?" – it remains radically **SUBJECTIVE**. If Hume is right, there is no answer to the question "why should I be moral?" or "why should I be benevolent?". If I don't want to be moral, that seems to be the end of the argument.

J.L. MACKIE Inventing Right and Wrong (1977) argues that the common view of moral language implies that there are some objective moral facts in the universe. But this view is a **MISTAKE**. There are no moral facts. We can only base our moral judgements on **FEELINGS** and **DESIRES**.

The **INTUITIONISTS** (G.E. Moore, H.A. Prichard, W.D. Ross) are arguing that there are **MORAL FACTS** but that we can only know them **NON-NATURALLY** as internal intuitions. This seems to be an attempt to have our cake and eat it.

R.M. HARE does have an answer to the question "why should I be moral?". At least in his later book **MORAL THINKING** Hare argues that people are more likely to be happy if they follow universal **PRESCRIPTIVISM** and reason from a viewpoint that takes into account the interests and preferences of all people affected by my decision. However, this is an appeal to **SELF-INTEREST** – Hare is still an **SUBJECTIVIST**.

Following **ANSCOMBE's** essay in 1958 the revival of Virtue ethics suggest a **NATURALIST** reason for being moral : we are moral to achieve personal and social **FLOURISHING**. If we can share the insights of psychology and philosophy we can come to a shared (if still **RELATIVISTIC**, cultural) view of what will build the excellent life. Naturalism has undergone a resurgence in the twentieth century, led by Geoffrey **WARNOCK** (1971, The Object of Morality) and Alasdair **MACINTYRE** (1981, After Virtue).

More recent, subtler, attempts to escape **SUBJECTIVISM** are to be found in John **RAWLS** A Theory of Justice, which asks us to assume the role of an avatar in a space ship, imagining we are in an **ORIGINAL POSITION** heading to a new world where we don't know our gender, intelligence, race, or circumstances. What rules would we formulate for this world? Rawls, like Hare, brings **KANT** back into the forefront of meta-ethical debate.

KEY QUOTES - META-ETHICS:

1. "That which is meant by "good" is the only simple object of thought which is peculiar to ethics". G.E. Moore

2. "As this ought expresses some new relation it is necessary that it should be observed and explained and at the same time that a reason be given". David Hume

3. "The use of "That is bad!" implies an appeal to an objective and impersonal standard in a way in which "I disapprove of this; do so as well!" does not. If emotivism is true, moral language is seriously misleading". Alasdair MacIntyre

4. "Good serves only as an emotive sign expressing our attitude to something, and perhaps evoking similar attitudes in other persons". A.J. Ayer

5. "To ask whether I ought to do A in these circumstances is to ask whether or not I will that doing A in these circumstances should become a universal law". R.M. Hare

6. "We have an idea of good ends that morality serves. Even if we are deontologists, we still think that there is a point to morality, and that point has to do with better outcomes – truth-telling generally produces better outcomes than lying. These ends can be put into non-moral language in terms of happiness, flourishing, welfare, or equality". Louis Pojman

Free will and Determinism

THE PROBLEM

If free will does not exist there can be no sense of moral **ACCOUNTABILITY**. Yet when we hold individuals accountable, we discover all kinds of psychological, genetic or environmental influences on human behaviour. How **FREE** then is the human will?

KEY TERMS

- **Voluntarism** – a human being makes a choice with no obvious constraint (limitation)

- **Positive freedom** – a power to act according to the determinants of the will

- **Negative freedom** – an absence of any obvious constraint

- **Hard determinism** – the will is caused by determinants (genetic and environmental) so strong that free will is an illusion

- **Compatibilism** (soft determinism) – free will is compatible with determinism

- **Libertarianism** – the will is free from causal determinants and subject to reason alone (Kant's view)

CASES IN HISTORY

In February 1993 two ten year old boys abducted a two year old child called Jamie **BULGER** from a shopping centre in Bootle, Merseyside. They took him to a railway track and brutally tortured and murdered him by dropping an iron bar on his head. He had 42 separate injuries. The judge Justice Morland described the case as one of "unparalleled evil and barbarity... In my judgment, your conduct was both cunning and very wicked."

But could a ten year old be held **MORALLY RESPONSIBLE**? Did they understand right and wrong? Some newspapers suggested the murderers were heavily influenced by the video nasty Child's Play 3. Do such influences affect our idea of responsibility? What of the **UPBRINGING** of the two children?

There are echoes in the Bulger case of the case of **LEOPOLD** and **LOEB** in America in 1924. The lawyer **CLARENCE DARROW** successfully argued that the two murderers could not be held fully responsible because:

1. It was genetically predetermined.

2. They were influenced by reading **NIETSZCHE**.

> "This terrible crime was inherent in their organism, and it came from some ancestor...is any blame attached because somebody took Nietzsche's philosophy and fashioned his life on it?" Clarence Darrow

On 15 March 1999, the **EUROPEAN COURT OF HUMAN RIGHTS** in Strasbourg ruled by 14 votes to 5 that there had been a violation of Article 6 of the European Convention on Human Rights regarding the fairness of the trial of Thompson and Venables, stating: "The public trial process in an adult court must be regarded in the case of an 11-year-old child as a severely intimidating procedure", and that Home Secretary **MICHAEL HOWARD's** decision to double the sentence from 8 to 15 years was also a denial of the two children's rights.

It seemed the European Court took the view that children could not be held fully responsible.

JOHN LOCKE's ANALOGY – the Truman Show

In defining freedom we need to distinguish between **VOLUNTARY** behaviour and **FREE** behaviour. This is because true freedom seems to be a deeper thing. It involves a **POWER** to make real choices, something stronger than the **ABSENCE OF CONSTRAINT**.

John Locke produced an analogy of the person in a locked room who prefers to stay quite voluntarily in the room not realising that the door is locked. The person **VOLUNTARILY** remains, but is actually **POWERLESS** to leave as the room is locked. So, concludes Locke, **FREEDOM** is more than **VOLUNTARINESS**. We may ask in the **BULGER** case: were Thompson and Venables **FREE** even though they were acting **VOLUNTARILY**?

Updating Locke, a woman may be **BRAINWASHED** (see the next chapter on **BEHAVIOURISM**) by society into believing, for example, that her proper place is in the home serving a dominant husband, not realising true freedom lies beyond the door. Try to leave the servitude (locked room) and she would find her husband and relatives blocking the door (for example, putting her under severe emotional pressure to stay). Is she truly free?

> "If a man is in a locked room and prefers his stay to going away… he has not freedom to be gone… so that liberty is not an idea belonging to volition…. But to the person having the power of doing according to the mind shall choose". John Locke

The **TRUMAN SHOW** depicts a world constructed as a huge TV set, controlled from a producer sitting in a fake moon in a staged sky. Truman cannot leave this constructed village. As long as he is happy in his illusion, he lives his life as an apparently free person even though the responses of all the characters are scripted and hence **PREDETERMINED**. He co-operates voluntarily to begin with. But in the deeper sense he cannot be described as **FREE**. The producer, when challenged, justifies this imprisonment: "Truman prefers his cell".

Truman is there **VOLUNTARILY** (for most of the film before he breaks out of the locked room). But he isn't free to leave – in fact when he tries to sail away in a boat, the producer attempts to kill him by generating a storm.

HARD DETERMINISM

Hard determinists take a **MECHANISTIC** view of the world. Science proves that every event has a cause.

The will must have a predetermined cause – a **FEELING** from inside or a determinant from outside (such as a friend's suggestion).

That pre-cause must have a preceding cause.

The chain continues way back into childhood – and if we could connect this chain we would realise that **FREE WILL** is an **ILLUSION**.

A contemporary hard determinist is Ted **HONDERICH** who believes "there can be no such hope if all the future is just an effect of effects". We must abandon **HOPE** of fashioning our future therefore because:

> "States of the brain are, in the first place, effects, the effects of other physical states... all actions are movements caused by **STATES OF THE BRAIN**".

LIBERTARIANISM

Kant argues that "freedom is the only one of all ideas in the speculative reason of which we know the possibility a priori - before experience - (without, however, understanding it) because it is a condition of the moral law which we know". Critique of Practical Reason

Kant divides the world into two realms. The **NOUMENAL** realm is the realm of ideas or **THINGS-IN-THEMSELVES**. These abstract ideas come before experience: we have the concept of **NUMBER** before we learn to **COUNT**. Kant sees the **PHENOMENAL** world, the part we share with animals, as ruled by passions and instincts which are not rational. The **WILL** belongs to the metaphysical world of the **A PRIORI**. As long as we act according to **REASON**, we are free.

> "The will, in the phenomenal sphere, is subject to the law of nature, and in so far, not free, and on the other hand, as belonging to the thing in itself, it is not subject to that law, and so, is free". Kant

HOW DO WE MAKE SENSE OF THE NON-DETERMINED WILL?

Kant's non-determined, metaphysical will suffers from the **INTELLIGIBILITY** problem:

INTELLIGIBILITY problem can be explained in this way:

1. If determinism is false, then events are not subject to chain of cause-and-effect.

    - So events occur randomly, by chance (**INDETERMINISM**).

    - If events occur by chance, then they are not under our control.

    - So, how can we be free and responsible?

2. Answer – **AGENT CAUSATION**

nselves
n and

I'm a hard determinist on principle

y
to

"A st
man".

d by a

COMPATIBILISM

The first two approaches to the free will debate are both **INCOMPATIBILIST**. They argue that free will cannot be reconciled with determinism.

Where **LIBERTARIANS** deny material causation of the human will and see it as **METAPHYSICAL**, **HARD DETERMINISTS** take a mechanistic view of the will as locked into a chain of pre-causes, so not free. A third way is **COMPATIBILISM**, the view that free will is compatible with determinism.

1. Human freedom cannot be understood without **DETERMINISM** because our choice is one of the causal factors.

2. Most human choices are a combination of **EXTERNAL** causes and an **INTERNAL ACT** of volition or will.

3. **COMPATIBILISTS** believe that freedom and responsibility are in every significant sense compatible with determinism; thus there is no conflict between determinism and free will.

4. **SOFT DETERMINISTS** are compatibilists who believe determinism is true.

    - **CLASSICAL** compatibilists include Hobbes, Hume, Mill

    - **MODERN** compatibilists include Ayer, Dennett, Frankfurt, Kane

DAVID HUME'S CLASSIC DEFENCE OF COMPATIBILISM

VOLUNTARY action only makes sense because there is a necessary connection between motive, desire, choice and action.

> "By liberty we mean a power of acting or not acting according to the determinations of the will". David Hume

EVERY ACT HAS TO BE CAUSED

Hume argued that every act has to be caused, otherwise it's **CHANCE**, not freedom. **NECESSITY** is Hume's word for determinism. The opposite of freedom says Hume isn't determinism, but constraint. In saying the opposite of freedom is determinism we are arguing that freedom is the same as **INDETERMINISM** – the uncaused will. But this makes freedom equivalent to randomness and chance.

> "Had not objects a regular conjunction with each other, we should never have entertained any notion of cause and effect....liberty when opposed to necessity, not to constraint, is the same thing with chance". Enquiry into Human Understanding

So freedom **REQUIRES** determinism to escape randomness. An uncaused action would be random and unpredictable, whereas human personality is **PREDICTABLE**. Human **MOTIVE** can be clearly established (and guilt requires we identify a **MOTIVE**).

> "These motives have a regular and uniform influence on the mind, and produce good and prevent evil actions...as motive is usually conjoined with action it must be esteemed a cause, and must be looked on as an instance of that necessity, which we would here establish". David Hume

CONTEMPORARY COMPATIBILISM: ROBERT KANE

Kane believes in five freedoms, and that we experience deep freedom particularly at times of struggle – when we feel ourselves torn between two choices. The five freedoms are:

1. **Self-realisation**

2. **Rational self-control**

3. **Self-perfection**

4. **Self-determination**

5. **Self-formation**

This final freedom allows us to act in a way not determined by our existing character: we can **CHOOSE TO CHANGE**.

> "Now I believe that such self-forming choices or actions occur at those difficult times of life when we are torn between competing visions of what we should do or become…we are faced with competing motivations and have to make the effort to overcome the temptation to do something else…the outcome is not determined because of the preceding indeterminacy – and yet it can be willed either way owing to the fact that in such self-formation the agent's prior wills are divided by conflicting motives". Robert Kane, Contemporary Introduction to Free Will

THE CHALLENGE FOR COMPATIBILISTS

INCOMPATIBILISTS (ie hard determinists and libertarians) say: for our actions to be free, it must be the case that, when we act, we **COULD DO OTHERWISE** than we actually do. This insistence on the ability to do otherwise is often referred to as the "principle of alternate possibilities".

The Classic **COMPATIBILIST** (Hume) replies: to say one 'could have done otherwise' is to say that one would have done otherwise had things been different (given a different set of beliefs, desires, etc.). But things were not different, so the causes which created our actions are identifiable by the sort of person we are.

So what if I couldn't 'do otherwise'? The ability to do otherwise is not in fact required for **MORAL RESPONSIBILITY**, and so determinism is no threat to free will.

The proper contrast to freedom is not determinism, but **CONSTRAINT**/coercion. As long as we are not constrained, coerced or forced in our actions then we do what we will, and it doesn't matter whether our wills are determined or not. (See back to Hume's quote).

This can be criticised as producing a **WEAK** view of freedom, roughly meaning "absence of constraint". Kant calls compatibilism a **WRETCHED SUBTERFUGE** and William James calls it a **QUAGMIRE OF EVASION**.

CONCLUSIONS

In some this may seem like a sterile debate, but it matters, as Clarence Darrow showed in 1924, and the case of Jamie Bulger's murder in February 1993, it is crucial for our ideas of **MORAL RESPONSIBILITY** and accountability.

Determinism cannot, in the end, be proven, although we are finding out more about brain states every year and their determinants in genes and upbringing. It is a **METAPHYSICAL** question imposed on us by the **SCIENTIFIC** worldview and a belief in a **MECHANISTIC** universe of cause and effect. In fact the scientific **PARADIGM** is changing with the insights of **QUANTUM PHYSICS** and **HEISENBERG's UNCERTAINTY PRINCIPLE**.

If every event has a cause couldn't free will remain a special type of cause, even, as Kant suggested, a metaphysical one coming from our ability to **REASON** (as the human mind may remain elusively beyond science, just as perception remains mysterious and something more than brain waves and biology)?

PSYCHOLOGY and the insights of the **BEHAVIOURISTS** such as **J.B.WATSON** and **B.F.SKINNER** have much to teach us about the difference between **VOLUNTARY** and **FREE**.

KEY QUOTES - FREE WILL AND DETERMINISM

1. "Liberty is not an idea belonging to volition but to the person having the power of doing according to the mind shall choose". John Locke

2. "States of the brain are, in the first place, effects, the effects of other physical states… all actions are movements caused by states of the brain". Ted Honderich

3. "Self-forming choices or actions occur at those difficult times of life when we are torn between competing visions of what we should do or become". Robert Kane

4. "Liberty when opposed to necessity is the same thing with chance". David Hume

5. "Freedom is the only one of all ideas in the speculative reason of which we know the possibility a priori - before experience- (without, however, understanding it) because it is a condition of the moral law which we know". Immanuel Kant

Behaviourism

Behaviourist psychologists sought to establish how human behaviour is determined by our environment. They conducted experiments in animals and later humans to see if behaviour could be altered by **ASSOCIATION**s created in the mind, or by **REWARDS** to condition certain desired behaviour. Pavlov's dog (1901), Little Albert (1920), Skinner's box (1938) and the Milgram experiment (1961) all offer valuable insights into human behaviour and the free will debate.

Behaviourism features in Aldous Huxley's **BRAVE NEW WORLD** where children of lower castes are conditioned to dislike books, flowers and nature in order to voluntarily adopt their caste's lifestyle. It is also an important influence on **ADVERTISING** where positive associations are created in brand identity (often with nothing directly to do with the product).

KEY TERMS

1. **Biodeterminism** - the view that genes determine our behaviour and intelligence

2. **Operant conditioning** - the creation of a desired response in an operant through repeated rewards

3. **Reflex conditioning** - the creation of a reflexive response such as salivation by creating an association such as noise with food

4. **Reinforcements** - incentives to repeat a desired behaviour

CONDITIONING - J.B.WATSON (1878-1957)

Watson believed we enter the world as a blank slate. Our unique ways of behaving are a result of our environment and experiences.

Watson rejected Freud's concept of the unconscious as unscientific, and so untestable. He argued we should base theories on **OBSERVATION** alone.

Humans learn by a process of **CONDITIONING**. He believed you could take any child and turn them into whoever you wanted: "I'll guarantee to take anyone at random and turn them into the specialist which I select".

PAVLOV'S DOG: CONDITIONING RESPONSES

Some things a dog doesn't need to learn, called **UNCONDITIONED** reflexes. For example, a dog doesn't need to learn to salivate in the presence of food.

Pavlov's assistant gave the dog food and the dog learnt to associate food with the assistant. The neutral stimulus (the assistant) had become associated with the unconditioned stimulus (food), so triggering a **REFLEX** (salivating). Pavlov called this **PSYCHIC SALIVATION**.

Pavlov rang a bell every time he gave the dogs food and so the dogs began to associate the bell with food. When Pavlov removed the food and just rang the bell, the dogs carried on salivating.

So the neutral stimulus (the bell) had become a **CONDITIONED STIMULUS** producing a **CONDITIONED RESPONSE** (salivation) . Behaviour is learnt or conditioned according to associations in our environment and upbringing.

Human beings can widen their associations using their imaginations, as happened with **LITTLE ALBERT**.

LITTLE ALBERT

Watson attempted to show the same conditioning in **HUMANS** as Pavlov produced in animals. He took an 8 month old baby, little Albert, who previously had no fear of rats.

His neutral stimulus was a **LOUD SOUND** just behind Albert's head, which upset him. Every time the rat appeared, Watson made the loud sound.

Watson presented Albert with the rat on his own, with no noise of a metal bar, and Albert started crying.

Albert had learnt to associate the rat with the upsetting noise, producing a **CONDITIONED REFLEX** (crying). He also found that Albert **GENERALISED** his fear to all white furry objects.

> "Psychology as the behaviourist views it is a purely objective experimental branch of natural science. Its theoretical goal is the prediction and control of behaviour. Introspection forms no essential part of its methods, nor is the scientific value of its data dependent upon the readiness with which they lend themselves to interpretation in terms of consciousness. The behaviourist, in his efforts to get a unitary scheme of animal response, recognizes no dividing line between man and brute. The behaviour of man, with all of its refinement and complexity, forms only a part of the behaviourist's total scheme of investigation". J.B.Watson

SKINNER'S BOX

J.B.Skinner (1904-1990) created experiments on animals and birds to demonstrate how behaviour can be determined by **REWARDS** given to the **OPERANT** of a simple device in a **BOX**. For example, an experiment on pigeons gives a reward when the pigeon pecks a **GREEN** light that comes on (but not a red one). This is called **OPERANT CONDITIONING**.

Skinner concluded that we learn by positive and negative feedback. These feedbacks are called **REINFORCEMENTS**.

The more **POSITIVE** reinforcement we receive, the more we will voluntarily repeat that behaviour (praise, prizes, rewards, satisfaction). Remember the distinction in the **FREE WILL** debate between **VOLUNTARY** and **FREE** behaviour. The pigeon chooses to peck the green light (it isn't **FORCED** – so **VOLUNTARY**), but is it **FREE**?

By operant Skinner means " an animal or human freely choosing a reward". So **OPERANT CONDITIONING** means causing **VOLUNTARY** repeat behaviour patterns in the operant just before a stimulus occurs.

Skinner put rats in a cage When the rat accidentally pressed a bar on the wall, a food pellet (the **REINFORCER**) was released. In no time the rat was furiously tapping away at the bar. If you stop giving pellets the rat quickly stops pushing the bar. The rat resumes its behaviour much more quickly when the pellets are reintroduced. It has learned by experience.

CONCLUSION

A behaviour followed by reinforcement **CAUSES** the behaviour to be repeated. If the reinforcement is withdrawn, the behaviour diminishes. The behaviour is **PRE-DETERMINED**.

So frequency and nature of **REINFORCEMENTS** are vital to sustain a desired behaviour. Skinner responded to criticisms that his theory took away human free will. What do we mean when we say we want to be free? Skinner said "we don't want to be punished for doing what we want".

So, Skinner argued, avoid negative reinforcements (punishment) and use only **POSITIVE** reinforcers to control society. Then we will feel free because we feel we are doing what we want! If you want to improve your child's behaviour **PRAISE** don't **BLAME**.

Skinner thought free will, consciousness, the unconscious were **"MENTALIST CONSTRUCTS"**, unobservable and so useless for scientific enquiry.

The problem with society, he argued, is that our positive and negative reinforcers are out of our control. Governments need to take control of society so good is rewarded and bad punished, so we can "design our culture" by **OPERANT CONDITIONING**.

BIODETERMINISM - FRANCIS GALTON (1822-1911)

Biodeterminism was highly popular in America in the early twentieth century. The state of **INDIANA** passed an enforced sterilisation law in 1907, and 2,500 people in prison were forcibly sterilised from 1907-1909. The final sterilisation law was only repealed in 1974. Biodeterminism found a terrible outlet in the **NAZI EUGENICS** programme following the 1934 **GENETICS** law allowing forced sterilisation. The poor, mentally ill, depressed were first sterilised and later gassed.

Galton aimed to "improve the racial qualities of future generations, whether physically or mentally". He wrote "we might introduce into the world prophets and high priests of civilisation, as surely as we can produce idiots by mating cretins".

He chillingly anticipated Nazi **EUGENICS** experiments, by arguing that "the feebler nations of the world are necessarily giving way before the nobler varieties of mankind".

GENES and DETERMINISM

Only 0.2% of human genetic makeup determines human differences e.g. skin colour. Humans have 30,000 genes, but chimps have only 2% difference in **DNA** sequence. Can a small genetic difference explain a large **BEHAVIOURAL** change, or differences in **INTELLIGENCE**?

Some geneticists believe sexual orientation, intelligence, criminality, aggression and addiction can be traced to the **GENOME**.

HARD DETERMINISTS believe genes control all human action and free will is an illusion. By voluntary selective breeding (engaged couples volunteered for a **DNA** test) in the 1980s a New York Jewish community entirely eradicated an inherited disease.

Diseases such as **HUNTINGTON**'s disease, which brings on presenile dementia, has been proved to be entirely genetic, and some evidence suggests violent criminals have an extra male chromosome **XYY**.

RICHARD DAWKINS' VIEW

Genes interact with the environment in a **DYNAMIC** way. So Richard Dawkins argues humans have developed an altruistic (kindness) gene and "are able to transcend their selfish genes".

Children from unstable and violent homes show different brain development. So human personality seems to be a complex **INTERACTION** between genes and environment.

Craig **VENTNER**, who mapped the genome in 2000, argues that "we simply don't have enough genes for biological determinism to be right. Our environments are critical".

Others fear that social inequality will eventually transfer to genetic inequality, with the creation of an "inferior" human, as in the film **GATTACA**.

> "Nature is organic, dynamic and interconnected. There are no linear causal chains linking genes and characteristics of organisms, let alone the human condition. The discredited paradigm is perpetuated by a scientific establishment consciously or unconsciously serving the corporate agenda". Science and Society

THE MILGRAM EXPERIMENT

In 1961 Stanley **MILGRAM** invited people to take part in a supposed MEMORY experiment. They believed that the person behind a glass panel was being subjected to electric shocks when they failed a simple memory test. In fact the subject was an actor and the experiment was designed to establish how many people would continue to administer electric shocks to the fatal dosage, simply because a scientist told them "it is **ESSENTIAL** the experiment continues".

Scientists wanted to find out why good people do terrible things. **EICHMANN** was put on trial in Israel for war crimes in 1962, claiming in his defence he was "simply following orders". Eichmann even argued he was following **KANT**'s categorical imperative "duty for duty's sake".

66% of participants administered levels of electric shock that can kill. It seemed the presence of an **AUTHORITY** figure overrode their **CONSCIENCE**. How could this coerced will be said to be **FREE**? Were the Milgram participants actually **RESPONSIBLE**?

The personality types which were quieter, mild-mannered and pleasant seemed more likely to co-operate. Milgram concluded that given the right **SITUATION** anyone could behave like a **MONSTER**.

Milgram concluded: "Ordinary people simply doing their jobs and without particular hostility on their part, can become agents in a terrible destructive process. When they are asked to carry out actions incompatible with fundamental standards of morality, relatively few people have the resources needed to resist authority".

Conscience

ISSUES

There are three major issues in a study of conscience.

1. What is the **ORIGIN** of conscience: does it come from God, our upbringing or from reason?

2. What is conscience, how does it **WORK**: is it a **MENTAL PROCESS** or part of our **REASON**, or a **FEELING**, or a **VOICE** in our heads (the voice of God?)?

3. Can we go against our conscience and choose to reject it, in other words, is conscience **FALLIBLE** and so likely to make mistakes, or is it inerrant (incapable of error)?

KEY TERMS

- **Conscientia** – Aquinas' term for reason guiding our actions, or "reason making right decisions"

- **Synderesis** – Aquinas' term for innate conscience, the tendency humans possess to "do good and avoid evil", also used by Paul eg in Romans 2:14 where he argues conscience is "woven into the very fabric of our creation"

- **Authoritarian conscience** – Eric Fromm's term used to describe a conscience which follows an authority figure

- **Superego** – Freud's term for conscience derived from parental praise and blame

THE PSYCHOLOGY OF CONSCIENCE – FREUD and PIAGET

CONSCIENCE AS GUILT - SIGMUND FREUD (1856-1939)

An alternative approach to conscience comes from Sigmund Freud. In his book, "The Outline of Psychoanalysis", (1949) he wrote that the human psyche is inspired by powerful instinctive desires that demand satisfaction.

These desires surface at our birth and are critical to our behaviour up to the age of 3 years. These overriding desires and their satisfaction (for food and comfort, for example) drive the **ID**.

The **ID** develops two broad categories of desire, according to Freud. **EROS** is the life-instinct, which gives us the desires for food, self-preservation, and sex. **THANATOS** is the death-instinct, which drives desires for domination, aggression, violence and self-destruction. These two instincts are at war within the id, and need to be tempered by ego constraints and by **CONSCIENCE**.

Children learn that authorities in the world restrict the extent to which these desires are satisfied. Consequently, humans create the **EGO** which takes account of the realities of the world and society. The ego Freud referred to as the **REALITY PRINCIPLE**, because our awareness of self and of others is crucial to our interaction with the world around us, and is formed at the age of 3 to 5 years.

The **SUPEREGO** develops from 5 years onwards, which internalises and reflects disapproval of others. So when our parents praise or blame us, frown and smile, we absorb a sense of shame at disapproval, and pleasure at approval.

In this way the superego forbids certain actions and produces a sense of GUILT. The Freudian model of the psyche is like an iceberg where most of the determinants are **SUBCONSCIOUS**.

The **SUPEREGO** grows into a life and power of its own irrespective of the rational thought and reflection of the individual: it is programmed into us by the reactions of other people.

This 'superego', conscience, restricts humans' aggressive powerful desires (**THANATOS** within the id) which would otherwise **DESTROY** us. So guilt "expresses itself in the need for punishment" (Civilisation and its Discontents 1930:315-6). Eric Fromm, quoting Nietzsche, agrees with Freud's analysis of the destructive nature of the **AUTHORITARIAN** conscience.

> "Freud has convincingly demonstrated the correctness of Nietzsche's thesis that the blockage of freedom turns man's instincts 'backward against man himself'. Enmity, cruelty, the delight in persecution...- the turning of all these instincts against their own possessors: this is the origin of the bad conscience". Eric Fromm, Man For Himself, 1947:113

Our superego can lead us to **INTERNALISE** shame, and to experience conflicts between the id desires and the shame emanating from the superego responses. The more we suppress our true feelings, the more that which drives us comes from what Freud described as the **SUBCONSCIOUS**, which like an iceberg lies hidden in the recesses of our minds.

A CASE STUDY

The former England footballer, Paul Gascoigne, suffers from an obsession to tidy and order things, even in the houses of friends he visits. In his autobiography he recounts this story of what happened to him as a young child, which may explain this **PATHOLOGICAL** behaviour.

> "One day, when I was ten, I took Keith's little brother Steven with us, telling his mam I would look after him. I was mucking about in the shop when Steven ran out into Derwentwater Road in front of a parked ice-cream van. He didn't see an oncoming car and it went right into him.
>
> I ran out and stood in front of the crumpled little body, screaming, 'Please move! Please move!'. His lips seemed to move slightly, but soon he was completely still. ...I just had to sit there, watching him die". Gazza - My Story, page 28

PIAGET AND CHILD DEVELOPMENT

Later psychologists modified Freud's theory. They argued that conscience has a mature and immature dimension.

MATURE conscience is healthy and is identified with the ego's search for integrity. It is concerned with right and wrong, and acts dynamically and responsively on things of value.

The mature conscience looks **OUTWARDS** to the world and the future, developing new insights into situations.

The **IMMATURE** conscience comprises the mass of guilty feelings acquired from parental and school discipline. These feelings have little to do with the rational importance of the action. The immature conscience acts out a desire to seek **APPROVAL** from others instead of the principles and beliefs of the person.

Piaget experimented to try to discover how conscience develops. He found that up to the age of ten, children judge rightness or wrongness according to the **CONSEQUENCES** of an action (eg I pile baked bean tins behind a door, as they crash down they make a terrible noise. The younger child feels guilty). Older children begin to link rightness and wrongness with **MOTIVE** and intention. In the above example, the child did not want or intend to scatter the baked bean cans, so the older child reasons "I'm not guilty!"

EVALUATION

1. These psychological accounts of conscience undermine both Aquinas' and Butler's religious theories of conscience because conscience is **ENVIRONMENTALLY INDUCED** by upbringing, not innate.

2. Highly **DETERMINISTIC**, because humans are driven, according to Freud, by forces operating out of our subconscious minds.

3. **PSYCHOLOGY** doesn't rule out the possibility that God has some involvement with conscience (in originating a moral faculty, for example), but if environment operates so strongly on conscience the religious theories need reworking.

INNATE CONSCIENCE

St Paul argued that all human beings, Jew and Gentile (non-Jew), possessed an innate knowledge of God's law, written on our hearts. "I do not do the thing I want, the very thing I hate is what I do" he wrote in **ROMANS 7** and Gentiles have God's law "engraved on their hearts", (Romans 2:15).

John Henry **NEWMAN** (1801-1890) was an Anglican priest who converted to Rome. How could a good Catholic accept papal **INFALLIBILITY** and still follow his conscience? Newman describes conscience as the innate **VOICE OF GOD** and **ABORIGINAL** (= original or native) **VICAR OF CHRIST**.

> "It is a principle planted in us before we have had any training" argued Newman. Newman quoted the fourth **LATERAN COUNCIL** when he said "he who acts against conscience loses his soul".

JOSEPH BUTLER – INNATE CONSCIENCE THAT IS GUIDED BY REASON

Joseph Butler (1692-1752), former Bishop of Durham, believed human beings had two natural rational guides to behaviour: enlightened self-interest and conscience. Greeks like **EPICURUS** would have recognised the self-interest of the pursuit of **HAPPINESS**, but not the idea of an **INNATE** (inborn) disposition of conscience.

Butler believed we were naturally moral, and that conscience was the **SUPREME AUTHORITY** in moral actions. Morality was part of our human natures.

Human nature has a **HIERARCHY OF VALUES** with conscience at the top which than adjudicates between the self-love and **BENEVOLENCE** (= doing good to others) which define us as human beings.   Conscience helps the selfish human become virtuous and so provides a **BALANCE** between these two tendencies.

Butler doesn't deny we have feelings and passions, but it is conscience which **JUDGES** between them as the "moral approving and disapproving faculty" and we act **PROPORTIONATELY** (appropriately to the situation) according to our conscience.

The guidance is **INTUITIVE**, given by God but still the voice of **REASON**. He is arguing that each human being has direct insight into the **UNIVERSAL** or objective rightness or wrongness of an action.

EVALUATION OF BUTLER

1. Butler attacked the **EGOISM** of Thomas Hobbes. **BENEVOLENCE** is as much part of our shared human nature as **SELF-LOVE**. Here there are echoes of Richard **DAWKINS**' argument that we all share a biologically evolved "altruistic gene" (altruism = concern for others).

2. Butler sees an **OBJECTIVE MORAL ORDER** on the world. Fortune and misfortune are not entirely arbitrary – if we choose **VICE** we naturally suffer misfortune. Following the dictates of conscience usually leads to **HAPPINESS**. But in the end it's **GOD** who guarantees the consequences turn out best.

3. "Although Butler's description of conscience is **UNSURPASSED**, he gives no definition of conscience". D.D.Raphael

> "Common behaviour all over the world is formed on a supposition of a moral faculty; whether called conscience, moral reason, moral sense, or divine reason; whether considered as a sentiment of understanding, or as a perception of the heart". Joseph Butler

JOHN HENRY NEWMAN AND CONSCIENCE

Cardinal John Henry Newman also took an **INTUITIONIST** approach. He wrote that "conscience is a law of the mind ... a messenger of him, who, both in nature and in grace, speaks to us behind a veil, and teaches and rules us by his representatives. Conscience is the aboriginal (ie original or natural) vicar of Christ." (John Henry Cardinal Newman, Letter to the Duke of Norfolk).

Newman believed that following conscience was following **DIVINE LAW**. Conscience is a messenger from God, and it is God speaking to us. Newman was a devout Catholic, but said in a letter 'I toast the Pope, but I toast conscience first'.

Catholics are obliged to do what they **SINCERELY BELIEVE** to be right even if they are mistaken. In a commentary to the Vatican documents, a brilliant young theologian named Joseph Ratzinger (now Pope Benedict) seems to agree.

> "Over the Pope as the expression of the binding claim of ecclesiastical authority there still stands one's own conscience, which must be obeyed before all else, if necessary even against the requirement of ecclesiastical authority". Pope Benedict

What happens where individual conscience comes up against **MORAL ABSOLUTES**, such as the absolute condemnation of abortion and contraception. The Church teaches that using artificial contraception is intrinsically wrong because it breaks the **INTRINSIC** link between sex and reproduction. Yet many couples ignore this teaching and maintain the inherent goodness of birth control to limit population growth, or maintain choices over careers.

So the Roman Catholic Church's teaching on conscience reflects both Newman and Aquinas and it holds that conscience is the law that speaks to the heart: 'conscience is a law written by God'. Gaudium et Spes

AUTHORITARIAN CONSCIENCE: ERIC FROMM

Eric Fromm experienced all the evil of Nazism and wrote his books to reflect on how conscience and freedom can be subverted even in the most civilised societies. In order to explain how, for example, Adolf **EICHMANN** can plead at his trial for mass murder in 1961 that he was only "following orders" in applying the final solution, we can invoke Fromm's idea of the authoritarian conscience.

The authoritarian conscience is the **INTERNALISED VOICE** of the external authority, something close to Freud's concept of the superego considered above. It's backed up by fear of punishment, or spurred on by admiration or can even be created because I idolise an authority figure, as Unity **MITFORD** did Adolf Hitler.

As Unity found, this blinds us to the faults of the idolised figure, and causes us to become **SUBJECT** to that person's will, so that "the laws and sanctions of the externalised authority become part of oneself" (1947:108).

So, as with the Nazis, ordinary seemingly civilised human beings do **ATROCIOUS EVIL** because they are subject to a voice which comes essentially from outside them, bypassing their own moral sense. This authoritarian conscience can come from:

1. **PROJECTION** onto someone of an image of perfection.

2. The experience of parental **RULES** or expectations.

3. An adopted **BELIEF** system, such as a religion, with its own authority structure.

> "Good conscience is consciousness of pleasing authority, guilty conscience is consciousness of displeasing it". Eric Fromm (1947:109)

The individual's **IDENTITY** and sense of security has become wrapped up in the authority figure, and the voice inside is really someone else's voice. This also means **OBEDIENCE** becomes the cardinal virtue, and as the Nazi Adolf Eichmann pleaded at his trial. **AUTONOMY** and **CREATIVITY** are lost.

> "Those subject to him are means to his end and, consequently his property, and used by him for his purposes." Fromm (1947:112)

DESTRUCTIVE TENDENCIES emerge, Fromm stresses, where "a person takes on the role of authority by treating himself with the same cruelty and strictness" and "destructive energies are discharged by taking on the role of the authority and dominating oneself as servant". (1947:113)

> "Paradoxically, authoritarian guilty conscience is a result of feelings of strength, independence, productiveness and pride, while the authoritarian good conscience springs from feelings of obedience, dependence, powerlessness and sinfulness". Fromm (1947:112)

THE HUMANISTIC CONSCIENCE

> "Different from the authoritarian conscience is the "humanistic conscience"; this is the voice present in every human being and independent from external sanctions and rewards. Humanistic conscience is based on the fact that as human beings we have an intuitive knowledge of what is human and inhuman, what is conducive of life and what is destructive of life. This conscience serves our functioning as human beings. It is the voice which calls us back to ourselves, to our humanity". Eric Fromm

The **HUMANISTIC** conscience is "our own voice, present in every human being, and independent of external sanctions and rewards" (1947:118). Fromm sees this voice as our **TRUE SELVES**, found by listening to ourselves and heeding our deepest needs, desires and goals.

The result of so listening is to release **HUMAN POTENTIAL** and creativity, and to become what we potentially are; "the goal is productiveness, and therefore, happiness" (1947:120). This is something gained over a life of learning, reflection and setting and realising goals for ourselves.

Fromm sees **KAFKA**'s "The Trial" as a parable of how the two consciences in practice live together. A man is arrested, he knows not on what charge or pretext. He seems powerless to prevent a terrible fate - his own death - at the hands of this alien authority. But just before he dies he gains a glimpse of another person (Fromm's other , **HUMANISTIC CONSCIENCE**) looking at him from an upstairs room.

CONSCIENCE AS THE POWER OF REASON

Aquinas (1224-1274) distinguished between an innate source of good and evil, **SYNDERESIS** (literally, one who watches over us) and a judgement derived from our reason, **CONSCIENTIA**.

In synderesis, Thomas Aquinas saw conscience as an innate instinct for distinguishing right from wrong. Synderesis can be defined as:

> "A natural disposition of the human mind by which we instinctively understand the first principles of morality". Aquinas

Aquinas (optimistically) thought people tended towards goodness and away from evil (the **SYNDERESIS** principle). This principle is the starting point or FIRST PRINCIPLE of Aquinas' **NATURAL LAW** system of ethics.

CONSCIENTIA as the power of reason for working out what was good and what was evil, the "application of knowledge to activity". This is something closer to moral judgement rather than instinct, close to Aristotle's **PHRONESIS** or practical wisdom. We cannot flourish without it. In practical situations we have to make choices and to weigh alternatives, and we do so by using our conscience.

Conscience can make mistakes and needs to be trained in wisdom. At times people do bad things because they make a mistake in discriminating good from evil. Aquinas believed that if the conscience has made a **FACTUAL** mistake, for example, if I don't realise that my action breaks a particular rule, then my mistaken conscience is not to blame.

But if I am simply **IGNORANT** of the rule (such as not committing adultery), I am to blame. Taking a rather bizarre example, Aquinas argues that if a man sleeps with another man's wife thinking she was his wife, then he is not morally blameworthy because he acted "in good faith".

> "Conscience is reason making right decisions and not a voice giving us commands". Aquinas

Conscience deliberates between good and bad. Aquinas notes two dimensions of moral decision making, "Man's reasoning is a kind of movement which begins with the understanding of certain things that are naturally known as **IMMUTABLE** principles without investigation. It ends in the intellectual activity by which we make judgements on the basis of those principles". Aquinas

So Synderesis is right **INSTINCT** or habit, the natural tendency human have to do good and avoid evil. Conscientia is right **REASON**, which distinguishes between right and wrong as we make practical moral decisions.

KEY QUOTES - CONSCIENCE

1. "Freud has convincingly demonstrated the correctness of Nietzche's thesis that the blockage of freedom turns man's instincts 'backward against man himself'. Enmity, cruelty, the delight in persecution...- the turning of all these instincts against their own possessors: this is the origin of the bad conscience". Eric Fromm

2. "Conscience does not only offer itself to show us the way we should walk in, but it likewise carries its own authority with it, that it is our natural guide, the guide assigned us by the Author of our nature; it therefore belongs to our condition of being, it is our duty to walk in its path". Joseph Butler

3. "Conscience is reason making right decisions and not a voice giving us commands". Aquinas

4. "The Gentiles (ie non-Jews) can demonstrate the effects of the law engraved on their hearts, to which their own conscience bears witness". Paul, Romans 2.15

5. "Conscience is the built in monitor of moral action or choice values". John Macquarrie

Virtue Ethics

Virtue ethics is the ethics of **CHARACTER**. What habits of character do I need to develop to build a good life? Its origins lie in Greek and Roman philosophy – **ARISTOTLE**'s Nichomachean Ethics (his lecture notes – fourth century BC) is particularly important. His works were preserved by Islam and discovered by Christians at the reconquest of **TOLEDO** in 1085.

AQUINAS (1227-74) then brought together Christian and Aristotelean insights in his **SUMMA THEOLOGICA** . **NATURAL LAW** and **VIRTUE ETHICS** should really be taught together: they are complementary, and share a common telos of **EUDAIMONIA** (flourishing or well-being). Aquinas adds **THEOLOGICAL VIRTUES** (faith, hope and love as in 1 CORINTHIANS 13) to more traditional ones (like the Greek virtues of courage, wisdom, temperance and fortitude).

KEY TERMS

1. **Arete** - Greek for virtue (skill, excellence are alternative words for virtue)

2. **Phronesis** - the Greek moral virtue of practical wisdom or prudence

3. **Sophia** - the Greek word for intellectual wisdom

4. **Eudaimonia** - the Greek word for flourishing or self-realisation (sometimes translated happiness)

5. **Golden mean** - Aristotle's idea of a judgement point between two vices, the vice of deficiency and the vice of excess, achieved by practical wisdom

6. **Temperance** - a key Greek virtue meaning moderation

FOUR CRITICISMS OF ACTION-BASED ETHICS

1. Action-based ethics cannot answer the question "why should I be moral?" Deontological ethics (eg **KANT**) focuses on negatives, on "thou shalt nots" looking primarily at the **INDIVIDUAL** but providing inadequate **MOTIVATION** to follow the rules laid down.

2. Action-based ethics are based on an outdated **THEOLOGICAL-LEGAL MODEL** of ethics. **NATURAL LAW** is based on **DIVINE LAW** coming from God where God is the **SOVEREIGN** ruler. **KANTIAN** ethics also focuses on rigid a priori **RULES**, with justice ultimately in the hands of **GOD** in the afterlife (the postulate of immortality).

3. Action-based theories ignore the spiritual dimension of ethics. Humans need to realise **POTENTIAL** and aspire to a range of emotional and spiritual goals, such as **INTEGRITY** and internal **PEACE**.

4. Action-based theories neglect the **COMMUNAL** basis of ethics. MacIntyre argues that Enlightenment philosophers like **KANT** overplay **AUTONOMY**. Ethics is rooted in community and shared practices and values. Virtues like **SYMPATHY**, kindness and friendship need strong communities to be expressed.

TELEOLOGICAL WORLDVIEW

The Greek worldview is **TELEOLOGICAL**. Everything has a true purpose (telos) sometimes called the **FINAL CAUSE**. The final cause (or aim or object) of good eating is health – the efficient cause (realising that aim) a nicely balanced diet. Louis Pojman explains it this way:

> "Humanity has an essence or a function. Just as it is a function of a doctor to cure the sick, and the function of a knife to cut well, so it is the function of humans to use reason in pursuit of the good life (eudaimonia). The virtues indicate the kind of political-moral characteristics necessary for people to attain happiness". Pojman (2006:161)

The final end of human life is to **FLOURISH** (**EUDAIMONIA** sometimes translated happiness but very different to Bentham's hedonic view). To flourish we need to build **MORAL** virtue through the practice of **PHRONESIS** (translated -prudence, judgement, practical wisdom), and **INTELLECTUAL** virtue (eg **TECHNE** or technical wisdom eg being good at **ICT**).

The goal is **EXCELLENCE** or good **SKILL**. So the Greek word for virtue (**ARETE**) means excellence, skill or habit. Rooney is an excellent (aretaic) footballer and Nelson Mandela an excellent (aretaic) person.

TWO WORDS for WISDOM (SOPHIA and PHRONESIS)

It's important to understand the two different words for wisdom in Greek, relating to the **CONTEMPLATIVE** and the **CALCULATIVE** mental processes.

INTELLECTUAL skills build **SOPHIA** - we can become a very wise scientist or literary critic. But the good **MORAL** character is built by (rather than builds – note the difference) **PHRONESIS** (the calculative intellectual skill of practical wisdom or right judgement).

So......

SKILL (PHRONESIS) + KNOWLEDGE (eg of IDEAL VIRTUES) = the GOOD LIFE (FLOURISHING)

There are three ways of gaining phronesis (three Es):

1. **EMULATE** your heroes (so heroism is important)

2. **EDUCATE** yourself (teachers are important)

3. **EXPERIENCE** life (think about your mistakes and learn from them)

No wonder Greeks respected the old and in Sparta the rule was by a small group of **PHRONIMOI** (wise men) – one of their jobs was to decide whether babies lived or were "exposed" on a hillside (male) or thrown off a cliff "female" because they were thought to be **WEAK**.

The virtuous character is built by **PHRONESIS** , the moral/intellectual virtue of practical wisdom – the skill of making decisions in difficult or different circumstances. Whereas **SOPHIA** is the end result of practising the intellectual virtues (such as **TECHNE**), phronesis is gained by exercising right moral judgement.

You can gain three As at A level – **SOPHIA** – but still act like a fool – lacking **PHRONESIS**. The excellent life requires both measures of wisdom.

VIRTUE as HABIT

Virtues need to be practised as habits until they become instincts, combining **REASON** and **EMOTION**. Over time we build a good character as a tree puts down roots and produces good fruit – and will need a good gardener (teacher) and soil (environment) to flourish (**EUDAIMONIA**).

This process needs **DISCIPLINE** – and it will be important to have good role models who show the virtues of **TEMPERANCE** and **FORTITUDE**. Rooney may be a skilful (**ARETE** – virtue or skill) footballer but he's a bad role model when he swears to the camera after scoring a hat-trick.

Part of postmodern confusion is that our **HEROES** are not good characters – so how are we to flourish if we follow **THEM**? Greek heroes had **FLAWS** – deliberately so (Achilles was jealous and childish), that's so we learn from their **VICES** as well.

GOLDEN MEAN

The **GOLDEN MEAN** is not a midpoint, but a judgement point somewhere between two vices, the **VICE OF DEFICIENCY** (lack of virtue) and the **VICE OF EXCESS** (too much virtue) which depends on the **SITUATION**.

That's why we need to develop the skill/virtue of **PHRONESIS** (right judgement). "Be angry for the right reason, with the right person, for the right length of time" said **ARISTOTLE** (how often the person getting mad is not really mad at you).

So the **VICE OF DEFICIENCY** is indifference (we should be very angry at genocide) and the **VICE OF EXCESS** is violent temper (anger can be inappropriate and we "lose it"). **PHRONESIS** makes the **APPROPRIATE** decision as we become wise and flourish, building **HABITS** that fulfil our potential (personal potential and also for society generally).

ABSOLUTE or RELATIVE

The list for virtues changes according to our **CULTURE** and time. So Spartans share with us a love of courage, but don't share with us their practice of killing the weaker babies, **INFANTICIDE**. They also practised slavery, were very liberated in some ways in their attitudes to women (who could own property) and believed you needed to kill a Macedonian to prove you were strong enough to be a warrior.

ARISTOTLE's list of virtues includes some familiar ones (courage, justice, temperance) and but also unexpected ones such as **MAGNIFICENCE** (close to the Christian vice of **PRIDE** meaning roughly buy the best not the cheapest). **AQUINAS** adds the **THEOLOGICAL** virtues of faith (faithfulness, trust), hope (persevering belief) and love (the Greek **AGAPE** or sacrificial, commitment love even for the stranger).

So virtues seem to be **RELATIVE** – but is there some **UNIVERSAL** virtue (friendship? courage? sympathy?) – which might indicate an element of **ABSOLUTE** morality as well?

MACINTYRE AFTER VIRTUE

Moral philosophy entered a dead end argues **MACINTYRE** when it lost sight of the **TELOS** of human action – the goal of **FLOURISHING** a naturalistic feature because it depends on human nature and **GOODS INTERNAL TO PRACTICES**. Morality makes sense within the roles we play in our own forms of life, with agreed, shared aims rules and obligations (family life, village life, company life, school life). When we know the **TELOS** (goal, purpose) of our form of life we will know what habits of character to develop to reinforce and strengthen it.

If we cannot agree on the **TELOS** (aim) then we cannot decide whether **KANT**'s ethics is better than **MILL**'s. The **ENLIGHTENMENT** shifted the emphasis from character to action. Then in the twentieth century **META-ETHICS** and the influence of **LOGICAL POSITIVISM/ EMOTIVISM** of **A.J. AYER** and others (Moore, Hare) began to dominate and questions of **MEANING** became the central focus of ethics (not, "am I a good person?" but, "what does good mean?").

The **NATURALISTIC FALLACY** was accepted as valid, whereas **MACINTYRE** argues agreement about a **TELOS** is an Aristotelean way of escaping the is/ought problem (where the goal or telos is eudaimonia - personal and social flourishing).

Modern naturalists like MacIntyre argue that as long as we can agree on the meaning of **EUDAIMONIA** (even if the view may change over time as psychology gives us new insight into the human condition), then we can escape the naturalistic fallacy. What is more, we can begin to answer the question posed by Socrates, but then abandoned by **EMOTIVISM**: "how then should we live?"

STRENGTHS

1. **HOLISTIC** view of human nature. Reason is applied through **PHRONESIS** or practical wisdom, but unlike Kant, the emotions are not ignored, as virtue ethics is holistic (includes emotion in the building of character). To Aristotle personal and social flourishing (**EUDAIMONIA**) is the final rational goal, and reason tames and moralises the desires and appetites of the irrational part of our soul.

2. **CHARACTER-BASED**. Habits of character are central, developed through **TRAINING**...we need heroes who are moral role models as well as virtuous (= skilful) footballers. The present age is "instrumental" in the sense of things being a means to an end, and **PRAGMATIC**, in that we tend to "bend the rules". Behind action lies character: it may be legal for an **MP** to claim expenses for a duck house, but is it honest?

3. **PARTIALITY** - Both Kant and Mill require impartiality for their ethical viewpoints, for example, Mill says "utilitarianism requires the moral agent to be strictly impartial, as a disinterested and benevolent spectator". James **RACHELS** comments: "it may be doubted whether impartiality is really such an important feature of the moral life...some virtues are partial and some are not. Love and friendship involve partiality towards loved ones and friends; beneficence (doing good) towards people in general is also a virtue...what is needed is not some general requirement of impartiality, but an understanding of how the different virtues relate to each other" (2007:173-4).

WEAKNESSES

1. **RELATIVISTIC** : we cannot agree what the key virtues are, which differ from culture to culture eg Al Qaeda thinks it is virtuous to be a suicide bomber. One person's terrorist is another person's freedom fighter and hero, so goodness must depend on something else. Perhaps we can escape this problem (as **MACINTYRE** argues we can) by defining what, for me or for my society, are the virtues which will make me (or us) **FLOURISH**.

"Aristotle saw pride as a special virtue, Christians see it as a master vice". Rachels (2007:166)

2. **DECISIONS** are difficult. "It is not obvious how we should go about deciding what to do" Rachels (2007:176) **ANSCOMBE** argues we should get rid of the idea of "right action" altogether and just use virtue words eg "unjust", "dishonest". William **FRANKENA** has argued "virtues without principles are blind", and virtues don't tell us where we get our principles. **RACHELS** argues that virtue ethics is incomplete because it can't account for the fact that "being honest" implies a rule, so "it's hard to see what honesty consists in if it is not the disposition to follow such rules". Rachels (2007:177).

3. **CONFLICTING VIRTUES**: What happens when virtues conflict, for example, when honesty and kindness conflict, or honesty and loyalty to one's friends? "It only leaves you wondering which virtue takes precedence", concludes Rachels. Louis **POJMAN** comments "virtue ethics has the problem of application: it doesn't tell us what to do in particular instances in which we most need direction". (2006:166)

CONFUSIONS

1. The **GOLDEN MEAN** means moderation. This isn't the case. Aristotle makes clear that it may be appropriate to show extreme anger in circumstances (think of cruelty or genocide for example). The mean is a judgement point which can only be fixed by t he **CIRCUMSTANCES**. It isn't a balance point.

2. Virtue ethics cannot handle moral decision-making. This argument is hotly disputed. Elizabeth **ANSCOMBE** argued that consequentialism couldn't handle decisions because of the impossibility of knowing the consequences, and deontology had lost its way in rules and regulations and "thou shalt nots". Virtue ethics, in stressing the learnt skill or right judgment, was the most practical way of reaching decisions as it retains a **FLEXIBILITY**. Fairness, for example, depends on a consideration of all relevant facts, not the application of a rule.

KEY QUOTES - VIRTUE ETHICS

1. "The soul of the students must be conditioned by good habits just as land must be cultivated to nurture seed". Aristotle

2. "We need to attend to virtues in the first place in order to understand the function and authority of rules". Alasdair MacIntyre

3. "Morality is internal and has to be expressed as 'be this' not 'do this'". Leslie Stephens

4. "We may even go as far as to say that the person who doesn't enjoy doing noble actions isn't a good person at all". Aristotle

5. "Virtue ethics is an ethics of aspiration, not an ethics of duty". Richard Taylor

6. "The mean and the best course is the course of virtue." Aristotle

7. ... that is

GOLDEN MEANIE

Business Ethics

INTRODUCTION

BUSINESS ETHICS is the critical examination of how people and institutions should behave in the world of commerce e.g. appropriate limits on self-interest, or (for firms) profits, when the actions of individuals or firms affect others. We may examine **CODES** which companies publish, or **BEHAVIOUR** of individuals – but also **CORPORATE CULTURE** (which may contradict the code) and responsibilities to the **ENVIRONMENT** and the developing world created by **GLOBALISATION** of markets and free trade between countries.

KEY TERMS

- **Profit motive** - the reward for risk-taking in maximising returns on any investment

- **Stakeholders** - any parties affected by a business practice

- **Externalities** - costs or benefits external to the company – pollution is a negative externality

- **Globalisation** - the interconnection of economies, information and culture

- **Multinationals** - companies that trade and pay tax in more than one country

ISSUES

1. Does the **PROFIT MOTIVE** conflict with ethical practice? Or does good ethics result in good business.

2. Should the regulation of business be left to **GOVERNMENTS**?

3. Ben and Jerry's has this **SOCIAL RESPONSIBILITY** statement at its heart: "to operate the company in a way that recognises the role business plays in the wider society and to find innovative ways to improve the life of the wider community". How widely is this view shared?

4. What happens when **STAKEHOLDER** interests conflict (eg sacking workers to raise shareholder returns?).

5. In a **GLOBALISED** world should we treat all workers the same irrespective of differences in national laws (think of safety regulations overseas)? Do **MULTINATIONALS** have too much power?

STAKE-HOLDERS

A **STAKEHOLDER** is any individual or group who has a stake in the success or failure of a company. It includes **INTERNAL STAKEHOLDERS** (managers, employees) and EXTERNAL (the local community, customers, shareholders, suppliers, local authorities, Government, other countries). For example, the existence of Tesco store may mean local shopkeepers do better (if more people visit the town) or worse (if business is taken away).

Stakeholder theory suggest we should consider the interests of all stakeholders in the consequences of a decision.

CODES

Most companies have **CODES OF ETHICS** which lay out the rights of different groups and the responsibilities and values of the company. **ETHICAL INVESTORS** only invest in companies that fulfil certain criteria eg **ENVIRONMENTAL** responsibility, and **FAIR TRADE** for overseas workers.

ETHICAL CONSUMERS look for sustainable sources or organic produce. The April 2011 riots in **BRISTOL** against the Tesco local store show how different interests may clash – stakeholders such as local businesses/some customers v. large corporations/ other customers and employees. Does Tesco have an **ETHICAL DUTY** not to destroy local businesses, or a duty to its potential **EMPLOYEES** (jobs) and **CUSTOMERS** (lower prices)? Is there and **ABSOLUTE** principle we can find to judge between them?

Most companies have ethics codes. But do they embody them as virtues?

COST/BENEFIT

COST/BENEFIT analysis is a business equivalent to **UTILITARIAN** ethics, as it seeks to weigh the benefits in money terms of a business decision against the cost. It suffers the same problem: the denial of **INDIVIDUAL RIGHTS** as a moral **ABSOLUTE**.

In the case of **FORD PINTO** (1970s) the cost of a **HUMAN LIFE** was weighed against the number of likely accidents and the cost of a **PRODUCT RECALL**. At $13 a car it was not worth the recall, they decided. But – they didn't calculate **CONSEQUENCES** correctly and valued **HUMAN LIFE** too cheaply – so ended up paying millions in compensation and having to **RECALL** the car anyway.

Unfortunately value has to be placed on a human life in traffic safety, **NHS** budgets etc – it's not economic to place a crash barrier alongside roads adjacent to remote reservoirs – so tragic accidents do occur (e.g in April 2011 four die in a car plunging into a reservoir in Wales).

If environmental costs are too high, will companies pay them or relocate their business?

EXTERNALITIES

EXTERNALITIES are costs paid (eg pollution) or benefits enjoyed(eg flowers in a roundabout) by someone external to the firm.

Traditionally Governments have taxed and regulated firms to make them comply with their ethical duties: **THE TEN HOURS ACT** (1847 restricts child labour to 10 hrs a day), the **CLEAN AIR ACT** (1956 restricts carbon emissions), the **HEALTH AND SAFETY ACT** (1974 – improved safety standards and penalised non-compliance), the **SEX DISCRIMINATION ACT** (1975 – Equal Pay and opportunity for women).

MILTON FRIEDMAN (economist) argues that companies have a duty only to their shareholders (ie profits) – it is for society to set the other ethical rules. But examples such as **ENRON**, the US energy company that went bankrupt in 2003 after massive fraud, indicate that laws are never enough – individuals need to take **RESPONSIBILITY**.

As environmental regulation increases the cost to companies rises. Yet the USA has still not signed up to immediate carbon emission reduction despite the 1996 **KYOTO** protocol and the **COPENHAGEN** (2008)and **DURBAN** (2011) summits. Although China, Russia and America signed the Durban agreement, this only committed countries to define a future treaty by 2015, which will be binding in 2020.Once again immediate action has been postponed. US Senator Jim Inhofe, who has called climate change "the greatest hoax every perpetrated on the American people", applauded the "complete collapse of the global warming movement and the Kyoto protocol".

RIGHTS

ABSOLUTISTS (eg Kantians) argue for universal human rights that apply everywhere for all time – including workers and communities in third world countries.

Because **GLOBALISATION** includes the free flow of **CAPITAL** to least cost countries, this can include those with corrupt governments or lax health and safety laws. Union Carbide (US firm) plant in **BHOPAL** (1986, India) and **TRAFIGURA** oil waste disposal (2008, Ivory Coast, hydrogen sulphide) illustrate how thousands can die (Bhopal – mustard gas) or go sick (Trafigura) when companies pursue least cost choices to boost **PROFIT**.

Worker and community rights often seem to take second place to **SHAREHOLDER** interests.

INDIVIDUALS

Individual workers may become **WHISTLEBLOWERS** and expose fraud, corruption, lax standards etc. The RBS sacked their finance director who "didn't fit in" = opposed their lending policy before the **GLOBAL FINANCIAL CRISIS**.

UK banks were 24 hours from collapse in 2008 before a Government rescue plan, in taking on their bad debts. The rescue of **ROYAL BANK OF SCOTLAND** cost £43bn. But in the **EUROZONE** crisis countries act like individuals, with David Cameron vetoing a recent treaty change because of **BRITAIN**'s **NATIONAL INTEREST**. Is there such an idea as **COLLECTIVE** (European) interest?

Individual **CONSCIENCE** may serve the **PUBLIC GOOD**, but at the cost of their own **SELF-INTEREST** (they're fired). Kantian and Natural Law ethics may help us cling to **ABSOLUTES**, but Utilitarian ethics tends to make us pragmatists as at the **NORMATIVE** level we lie or stay silent to serve a **COLLECTIVE** interest (and don't have enough sympathy with outsiders to care).

However **ENRON**'s collapse in 2003 brought down auditor **ARTHUR ANDERSEN** as it was implicated in the financial fraud which covered up huge debts, and affected shareholders, employees and pensioners. Sometimes **SHORT -TERMISM** in the calculation can have terrible long-term consequences, and the courage of **ERIN BROKOVITCH** in exposing the toxic leaks of **PACIFIC GAS** in an American town shows how **VIRTUE ETHICS** may have much to teach us in Business affairs.

FUTURE GENERATIONS

One of the puzzles of ethics is how we account for the interests of future generations and animals, plants, etc. **KANTIAN** and **NATURAL LAW** ethics are traditionally weak on environmental issues (Kant stresses rational autonomous beings as having moral worth, not animals, and Natural Law primary precepts never mentioned the Environment until **VERITATIS SPLENDOR** in 1995).

UTILITARIANISM in principle could do better – but how do we know how many people to add in to the calculation? How do we assess the environmental effect of the plastic bag "island" the size of Texas which exists in the central vortex of the **PACIFIC** ocean currents? **SUSTAINABLE DEVELOPMENT** is a new idea – and **CHRISTIAN ETHICS** has arguably suffered from an emphasis on **DOMINION** (Genesis 1:26) = exploit, rather than **STEWARDSHIP** = care for the environment.

Can we provide incentives to this generation to protect future rights of the unborn?

GLOBALISATION

Globalisation is the **INTERCONNECTION** of markets, technology and information across the world. There are said to be five global brands: Nike, Coca-Cola, McDonalds, Levi. However globalisation brings the risk that large companies dominate the political agenda working in their own interest, and also force wages down for third world suppliers. For example, multinationals fund **PRESIDENTIAL** campaigns and the oil industry lobbies ceaselessly to stop any rise in **OIL PRICES** and even, it has been alleged, the development or subsidy of alternative energy sources.

The economist Amartya Sen has argued that the central issue is "the **UNEQUAL SHARING** in the benefits of globalisation" – that the poor receive an unequal gain from any wealth created. Put another way, less developed countries are exploited for cheap labour in the global market place (compare **WAGES PER HOUR** in China and the UK for example).

Finally there is the question of **REGULATION**. Do multinationals export lax safety standards and poor environmental disciplines to the third world? The examples of **BHOPAL** (1984) and **TRAFIGURA*** (2007) are not encouraging. And could any government have stopped a deregulated world banking system bringing the world economy to the brink of collapse in the crisis of 2008? Short-term profit and excessive **RISK-TAKING** in property lending led to the accumulation of huge debts so that Royal Bank of Scotland was only saved from bankruptcy by a £43bn cash injection by the UK Government.

Are multinationals beyond state regulation? Do they have too much power? What incentive do they have to be ethical?

* In 2007 Trafigura established a foundation to promote environmental concern, rural development programmes and health programmes in the counties where it operated. So far $ 14.5 m dollars has been donated to 36 projects. It is now seeking to create "a lasting, sustainable model for corporate philanthropy".

Environmental Ethics

Environmental ethics considers the relationship between human beings and the **BIOSPHERE** (bios = life).

Key questions include:

1. Should human beings use natural resources purely for their own good (**INSTRUMENTAL** good) or is there something **INTRINSICALLY** good about the environment?

2. To what extent should we consider future generations (and can our ethical theories handle this idea?). What moral weight do we give the **UNBORN**?

3. What is the status of animals? Can animals have **RIGHTS**?

4. Do we have a moral obligation to conserve resources?

5. What does it mean to be human? Are humans superior to animals, with special rights?

THREE APPROACHES

1. **DEEP ECOLOGY** argues that the environment has intrinsic goodness because all life is interdependent. Examples include GAIA theory of James Lovelock of the **ECOHOLISM** of Arne Naess.

2. **SHALLOW ECOLOGY** argues that the environment has instrumental goodness as a means to the end of human happiness (for example in **UTILITARIAN** ethics)

3. **ANTHROPOCENTRIC** theories focus solely on humankind (for example **KANTIAN** Ethics).

SOME FACTS

According to **DAVID ATTENBOROUGH** (Life on earth 2008), the earth's temperature will rise between 1.4 and 5.8 degrees in 100 years. **PETER COX** argues "even 2 degrees would be a dangerous climate change...6 degrees would damage us irreparably". In the last 25 years ice cap the size of Texas has melted. "Up to half our natural species are under threat of extinction by 2,100" says Attenborough.

DEVELOPING COUNTRIES such as China grow by 10% per year and yet still emit only one seventh of American CO_2 per head. All the same, China is building two coal powered power stations a week. By 2050 world CO_2 emissions are set to **DOUBLE**.

If we have a 4 degree rise in temperature world **POPULATION** will likely decline by 90% due to food shortages. As in past temperature cycles a **MASS EXTINCTION** is possible. Lovelock argues that by 2,100 the population will be around 1 billion.

WHAT CAN WE DO?

Scientists speak of **TIPPING POINTS** after which there's no turning back.

1. **MELTING ICE CAPS** create new areas of dark water which absorb heat and so accelerate warming.

2. **DEFORESTATION** accelerates as rainforest is cut down and fails to regenerate due to rising temperatures, forest fires and erosion.

3. The **ACIDITY** of oceans rises, and as algae dies and fish stocks decline, the acididty becomes irreversible.

DEEP ECOLOGY and ECO-HOLISM: GAIA

- **QUESTION**: How interdependent is the biosphere?
- **ANSWER**: It is one interdependent system, like a single organism, or the human body itself.

James **LOVELOCK** originated Gaia Theory in the 1965, adopting the name of the Greek goddess of the earth. The idea has been developed further by **LYN MARGOLIS**.

> "The Gaia hypothesis views the biosphere as an adaptive control system able to maintain the earth in homeostasis...living organisms regulate the climate and chemistry of the atmosphere in their own interest". Lovelock (2007:29)

For a quarter of the time the universe has existed (3 billion years out of 12 billion), Gaia has produced a system of **SELF-REGULATION** where the temperature stays close to the ideal for flourishing life.

As temperature rises **FEEDBACK** mechanisms keep the earth in a **DYNAMIC EQUILIBRIUM**. For example, oxygen stays constant at 21% of the atmosphere. Recently this has been confirmed by the computer model known as the **DAISYWORLD** simulation.

> "In this world there are white and black daisies. Daisies absorb heat and they flourish in lower temperatures whereas white daisies reflect heat and flourish at higher temperatures. Therefore as the temperature of the world increases more white daisies grow and as they reflect heat thereby lowering the temperature this encourages more black daisies to grow and flourish. But as black daisies increase the temperature that they absorb heat this increase the temperature of the world which encourage the white daisies increase and the black daisies die out. This process carries on without stop and illustrates the world is in a state of equilibrium or homeostasis. Thus Gaia's self-regulation will likely prevent any extraordinary runaway effects that wipe out life itself, but that humans will survive and be culled and, I hope, refined".

So the earth is seen as one interdependent **HOLISTIC** life form. This holistic view rejects the **ONTOLOGICAL DUALISM** of inert **MATTER v SENTIENCE** in favour of a **MONISM** – all matter is seen as in some sense alive. There is no hierarchy with humankind at the top.

Lovelock describes Gaia as "a **PHYSIOLOGICAL** system because it seems to have the unconscious goal of regulating the climate and the chemistry at a comfortable state for life" (2007:20). **DAWKINS** rejects this purposeful view of nature. Gaia is however a **METAPHOR**: "it has never been more than a metaphor…no more serious than a sailor who refers to his ship as "she". Lovelock (2007:21)

Lovelock likens Gaia to a camel: "when forcing is too strong, whether to the hot or the cold, Gaia, as a camel would, moves to a new stable state that is easier to maintain. She is about to move now". (2007:21) Hence a recent book describes the **REVENGE** of Gaia. Lovelock predicts that the world population will fall from 7 to 1.5 billion.

Gaia theory accepts the idea of **EVOLUTION** but sees it as too limited. As in Darwinian theory organisms adapt to their environment. But in Gaia theory the organisms also contribute to and change the nature of the environment, so that organism and environment become interdependent: they evolve together. Now that the industrialised world has greatly accelerated the rate of environmental change, the question is, what effects will those accelerated changes have on the balance of biotic life?

> "It was a moment of personal revelation...in 1965...that I glimpsed Gaia..could it be that life on earth not only made the atmosphere, but also regulated it – keeping it at a constant composition favourable for organisms?" Lovelock (1991)

DEEP ECOLOGY and ECOSOPHY

- **QUESTION**: Are we doing enough to save the planet?

- **ANSWER**: We need a new morality with a new definition of what it means to be human. The new morality entails a new **POLITICS**, abandoning the goal of economic growth.

Arne Naess coined the phrase **DEEP ECOLOGY** in 1973 and argues that we will need deep experience (seeing the beauty of a glacier), deep understanding (of the science of climate and the biosphere) and deep commitment (to a new ecological manifesto). **ECOSOPHY** is "a complete system of being, thinking and acting in the world which takes into account ecological balance and harmony". Stephan Harding (2002).

Naess argues that "the right of all forms of life to live is a universal right which cannot be quantified. No single species of living being has more of this particular right to live and unfold than any other species". Naess (1973). There is no **HIERARCHY** with humankind at the top.

Warren Fox echoes this when he speaks of "all life as part of a single unfolding reality". (1990)

NAESS' POLITICAL MANIFESTO

1. Reduce population growth now.

2. Abandon economic growth as a goal.

3. Conserve diversity of species.

4. Live in small, self-reliant communities.

5. Touch the earth lightly and leave a light footprint.

NAESS and SISSONS' EIGHT PRINCIPLES OF DEEP ECOLOGY

1. All life has **VALUE** in itself, independent of its usefulness to humans.

2. Richness and diversity are good in themselves (**INTRINSIC GOODS**).

3. Humans may only reduce this richness and diversity to meet **VITAL NEEDS**.

4. The impact of human beings is **INCREASING** and must diminish.

5. **OVERPOPULATION** is a key factor in environmental destruction.

6. The diversity of life (an intrinsic good) is being **DIMINISHED** by human action.

7. Economic and political structures must **CHANGE** to meet the environmental challenge.

8. Those who agree need to **ORGANISE** and **ACT** now.

DEEP ECOLOGY and the LAND ETHIC: ALDO LEOPOLD

A Sand County Almanac, 1948

Leopold argues that humans are not naturally superior but simply part of one interdependent system. The biotic community has **INTRINSIC VALUE**. "A thing is right when it tends to preserve the integrity, stability and beauty of the biotic community. It is wrong when it tends to do otherwise". So land health and the welfare of the planet are ethically more significant than any other traditional concerns of ethics – such as human happiness.

Leopold called for a change in our **MENTAL ATTITUDE** – a new environmental **CONSCIENCE**. "The problem we face is the extension of the social conscience from people to the land". This new conscience involves emotions as well as new attitudes. It is a commitment to the whole person to the mystical elements of land – it's beauty, as well as it's function. We grasp this with **EMOTIONAL INTELLIGENCE** as well as rational intelligence. So Leopold challenges the **RATIONALIST** basis of much of western ethics.

We are part of a **COMMUNITY** which includes all things – all species, rocks, trees. "That land is a community is the basic concept of ecology, but that land it to be loved and respected is an extension of ethics".

Leopold rejects the traditional **DUALISMS** of man v nature or emotion v reason. Humans are not superior to other species and have no right of dominance over them.

Land is more than soil – it is a "fount of **ENERGY**". So there is a new concept of land not as resource or as property.

"Land, then, is not merely soil; it is a **FOUNTAIN OF ENERGY** flowing through a circuit of soils, plants, and animals. Food chains are the living channels which conduct energy upward; death and decay return it to the soil. The circuit is not closed; some energy is dissipated in decay, some is added by absorption from the air, some is stored in soils, peats, and long-lived forests; but it is a sustained circuit, like a slowly augmented revolving fund of life". Land Ethic page 216

Leopold deplores two tendencies – the exhaustion of the wilderness and the **HYBRIDISATION** of cultures. Cultural diversity and **BIOTIC DIVERSITY** were two moral goods which he saw wasting away.

So, he concludes, we need to rewrite history from an environmental viewpoint. "That man is, in fact, only a member of a biotic team is shown by an ecological interpretation of history. Many historical events, hitherto explained solely in terms of human enterprise [whether economic or ethical], were actually **BIOTIC INTERACTIONS** between people and land. The characteristics of the land determined the facts quite as potently as the characteristics of the men who lived on it".

EVALUATION OF DEEP ECOLOGY

1. The political agenda of zero economic growth and consensual population reduction is unrealistic. Democracy requires economic growth (otherwise **INSTABILITY** arises) and developing countries like China and India need to raise living standards.

2. The real issue with deep ecology is how to justify the claim that all parts of the created order have **RIGHTS**.

3. Deep ecology leaves the problem of deciding on priorities. How do we decide who or what is to be given **PRIORITY** when the interests of human and nonhuman creatures are incompatible? Even if animals and plants have rights, how are these to be balanced against human rights If it is decided to grant rights to plants and animals but not equal rights what by what criteria should they be conferred (consciousness, complexity, attractive appearance, good to eat, ability to feel pain, intelligence)?

4. If humans are not granted priority in a 'natural' situation, inhumanity could be justified; for example, if famine struck a country then deep ecology could be used to justify leaving the people within that country to die. It could be argued that it is better for the entire system, to allow this to happen. To allow the human population to die might allow animals and plant life to flourish unhampered, and within deep ecology they are of **EQUAL VALUE** to human life.

5. If a rain forest has 'rights', who has the responsibility to grant those rights? The country which has the rain forest may not be able to **PRESERVE** them without significant cost, which it may

not be able to afford. Cutting the rain forest may provide a vital source of land and income to a developing nation.

SHALLOW ECOLOGY: UTILITARIANISM and Peter Singer

- **QUESTION**: Do animals and the environment have rights?
- **ANSWER**: Animals have rights as sentient (feeling) beings (Singer). But any utilitarian rights are only **INSTRUMENTAL**, not absolute.

Duties to other creatures and non-human life are measured by a cost-benefit analysis. Some Utilitarians argue that there are ethical obligations to **FUTURE** GENERATIONS.

John Passmore advocates a '**SCIENTIFICALLY INFORMED** utilitarianism'. If we damage the biosphere we end up injuring ourselves. **POLLUTION** of air, water and land is detrimental to human health and harms human life, and is therefore morally wrong.

However **IF** we **COULD** damage the environment without harming human life it would not be regarded as morally wrong in itself.

Preserving wilderness and areas of outstanding natural beauty can also serve the greatest good for the greatest number principle – by maximising pleasure.

For human recreation (eg camping, fishing, hunting) but the enjoyment of natural beauty and its positive influence on human character are other less tangible benefits.

For its use in scientific research – for example cures for diseases may be discovered by experimenting with unusual plants in rain forests.

OBLIGATION TO FUTURE GENERATIONS

There may also be an obligation to preserve the environment for the **UNBORN**. Many environmental effects are long-term. By depleting resources and polluting the environment we are jeopardising the welfare of future generations.

The unborn need to be considered in sustainable use of resources (land, sea, forest).

The unborn need to be considered in the **EXTERNALITIES** generated by production and consumption – of oil and coal for example.

However whilst John Stuart Mill spoke of 'the general interest of the human race' he never applied the principle of the greatest good for the greatest number to future generations. For some Utilitarians there are no obligations to future generations. Calculation of cost/benefit will only include those currently living and the aim will be to create a balance of pleasure over pain for the many, even if this is at the expense of some humans and some animals and even if the predictions for future generations are not great.

Utilitarians require us to **PREDICT CONSEQUENCES** but Utilitarians disagree about how far into the future they must try and predict. If however the Utilitarian might feel pain – guilt perhaps – at not considering future generations then this would be added into the equation.

OBLIGATIONS TO ANIMALS

It is possible for a Utilitarian to argue that both animals and the environment have rights.

THE RIGHTS OF ANIMALS

Bentham and Mill held that we have **DUTIES TO ANIMALS**, because they have the capacity to suffer. Peter Singer in his book Animal Liberation (1995) follows this through to its logical conclusion by arguing for equal ethical responsibilities to all species that can experience pleasure or pain:

> "If a being suffers, there can be no moral justification for refusing to take the suffering into consideration. No matter what the nature of the being, the principle for equality requires that suffering be counted equally with the like suffering – in so far as rough comparisons can be made – of any other being If a being is not capable of suffering or of experiencing enjoyment or happiness, there is nothing to be taken into account". Peter Singer

Singer extends **BENTHAM**'s principle 'each to count for one and none for more than one' to animals. He argues that as far as they suffer pain they have interests and in this sense must be treated equally.

Singer's position would also mean no further experimentation on animals, as the animal can not give consent, and if medical science is to progress this would mean far more experimentation on human subjects who can give consent.

THE RIGHTS OF PLANTS

For most **UTILITARIANS** it would be acceptable to use the environment for the benefit of humans even if that resulted in the suffering of animals and damage to the environment. Robin **ATTFIELD** develops an expanded utilitarianism that includes the welfare of non-sentient living things, which means plants, and whole ecosystems. He claims that all living things have **INTERESTS** and innate capacities, which can be furthered or hampered by human action.

The goal of this approach is not the avoidance of pain but the promotion of well-being for all living things. There are Utilitarians who extent the circle of interest to mountains and rivers and the whole of the natural world.

EVALUATION OF SHALLOW ECOLOGY

1. Small human populations and small countries, such as the Maldives, could be allowed to disappear if the **COST** of preserving them seemed too high.

2. It is questionable whether human interest, even on a long time scale, provides strong enough reason to protect **OTHER SPECIES**. It could be acceptable within shallow ecology for an animal species to become extinct if no human good was served by preserving it. Animals do not have any intrinsic rights.

3. Placing human **WELFARE** at the centre may benefit the human population initially but may result in long term problems. Many ecologists argue that the survival of all species on the planet is related but the evidence for these claims may only become available when it is too late to.

ANTHROPOCENTRISM

Traditional moral theories are sometimes accused of being **ANTHROPOCENTRIC** (human being centred). The source and focus of moral value is in human beings, and not animals or nature. Often human life is seen as being **ETHICALLY SUPERIOR** to other life forms.

KANT

For Kant moral value comes from us being **AUTONOMOUS, SELF-LEGISLATING** beings. We are free, responsible and able to grasp the **CONSISTENCY** of moral thinking. Human beings have two elements to their natures: we share with **ANGELS** the ability to think in the abstract, in the world of ideas or **NOUMENAL** realm. We share with **ANIMALS** the passions, instincts and experiences of the **PHENOMENAL** realm, the realm of the passions. This gives us a clue about a defence of Kant and issues around the environment.

Christine **KORSGAARD** has argued that because we share some of our natures with animals we should universalise our decisions with animals in mind. How would it be for the whole **SENTIENT** world if all people behaved like this?

We could also argue that you can **UNIVERSALISE** any statement. So there is nothing logically incoherent about universalising the idea that we should not act in such a way as to degrade the environment. If we do, then we commit collective **SUICIDE**, in much the same way as we cannot envisage committing **INDIVIDUAL** suicide (Kant once argued).

NATURAL LAW

Natural Law theory sees five rational principles emerging from the general tendency to "do good and avoid evil" (the **SYNDERESIS** principle). One of these is **PRESERVATION OF LIFE**. Aquinas, however, said little about the environment and what he did say implied the **SUPERIORITY** of humankind. Echoing a more negative interpretation of **DOMINION** (Genesis 1:26), he argued that "according to the Divine ordinance the life of animals and plants is preserved not for themselves but for man. Hence, as Augustine says, "by a most just ordinance of the Creator, both their life and their death are subject to our use".

Recent papal documents have extended the primary precepts to include the environment. **VERITATIS SPLENDOR** (1995) adds **CONTEMPLATION OF BEAUTY** and stewardship of the environment as key ethical concerns.

"RELIGIOUS ETHICS IS THE BEST APPROACH TO THE ENVIRONMENT". DISCUSS.

Lynn **WHITE**'s article "The Historical Roots of our Ecological Crisis" argues that the current disaster facing the environment is due to the Christian command to have 'dominion' over the earth (Genesis). People have moved from nature-centred religions to a religion where God demands dominion over nature and with the curse requires that we till the ground and uproot the weeds. Only when the Christian view is rejected can the ecological crisis be solved.

White does acknowledge the 'whisper' of some enlightened individuals, such as **FRANCIS OF ASSISI** who treated all nature equally worthy of Gods faith, hope and love. But his voice is not enough:

> "The greatest spiritual revolutionary in western history, St Francis, proposed what he thought was an alternative Christian view of nature and man's relation to it; he tried to substitute the idea of the equality of all creature, including man, for the ideas of man's limitless rule of creation. He failed". Lyn White

CONFUSIONS

1. Traditional moral theories (Kant, Natural Law, Utilitarianism) cannot accommodate environmental issues. Not so. The Roman Catholic interpretation of **NATURAL LAW** includes "contemplation of beauty" and concern for the environment as its precepts (see **VERITATIS SPLENDOR** 1995).   Kantian ethics has been revised by modern Kantians such as Christine **KORSGAARD** to include environmental issues.

2. "Rights are nonsense on stilts" (Bentham). This isn't the case: rights are a social agreement about value (worth). We can give rights to animals eg the right not to suffer, the right of a species to survive. Such rights can come from **RELIGION** or **NATURAL LAW** or **RULE UTILITARIANISM**. They are derived a different way – but they do make logical sense.

KEY QUOTES - ENVIRONMENTAL ETHICS

1. "A thing is right when it tends to preserve the integrity, stability and beauty of the biotic community. It is wrong when it tends to do otherwise". Aldo Leopold

2. "The question is not, 'Can animals reason?' nor ' Can they talk?' but 'Can they suffer?'" Peter Singer

3. "In taking ourselves to be an end in ourselves we legislate that the natural good of a creature that matters to itself is the source of moral claims. Animal nature is an end-in-itself because our own legislation makes it so. And that is why we have duties to animals". Christine Korsgaard

4. "Dumb animals and plants are devoid of the life of reason whereby to set themselves in motion; they are moved, as it were by another, by a kind of natural impulse, a sign of which is that they are naturally enslaved and accommodated to the uses of others". Thomas Aquinas

5. "Gaia is stern and tough, always keeping the world warm and comfortable for those who obey the rules, but ruthless in her destruction of those who transgress. Her unconscious goal is a planet fit for life. If humans stand in the way of this, we shall be eliminated with as little pity as would be shown by the micro-brain of an intercontinental ballistic nuclear missile in full flight to its target". James Lovelock – The Ages of Gaia

Sexual Ethics

ISSUES SURROUNDING SEXUAL ETHICS

1. What does it mean to be human? Is there one universal shared human nature?

2. Are gender equality and same sex attraction equally ethical issues?

3. What values give meaning to sexual relationships (such as fidelity, chastity, commitment – which seem to be changing)? Are the **VIRTUES** a better way of analysing this issue?

4. How have developments in understanding the biology and **PSYCHOLOGY** of the human person affected sexual ethics?

Sexual ethics thus shares concerns and insights from **PSYCHOLOGY**, **BIOLOGY**, and **SOCIOLOGY**. With the prevalence of pornography, sex trafficking and decline in old models of family life, there can be few more pressing ethical issues facing us. At **A2** we study four issues:

1. **CONTRACEPTION**

2. **PRE-MARITAL SEX**

3. **ADULTERY**

4. **HOMOSEXUALITY**

SEX AND EVOLUTION

Homo Sapiens emerged around 150,000 years ago. As social life developed so a primitive **MORALITY** created rules and boundaries around sexual intercourse. Sex changes its function from **REPRODUCTION** to **SOCIAL REGULATION**.

Religions emerge that created **PURITY CODES**. These involved **TABOOS** (the declaration of certain practices as unclean). For example the purity code of the Hebrew Bible, **LEVITICUS**, lays down a code of uncleanness – which included **BLOOD, INCEST, ADULTERY**, and **SAME SEX RELATIONS**. These are abominations punishable by social exclusion or death.

Such attitudes are reflected in attitudes to **WOMEN**. Women came to be seen as **PROPERTY** of men. Virginity was prized. Up to 1872, married women in Britain had to surrender all property to their husbands; there was no concept of marital rape until 1991 and violence against married women was only outlawed in 1861. In 2011 there were 443 reported incidents of "honour crime" (violence, forced marriage and even murder) in the UK.

A concept of what is **NATURAL** emerged and with it psychological **GUILT** for those who did not conform. It's hard to believe that in 1899 **OSCAR WILDE** was jailed for two years hard labour for homosexual relationship. **HOMOSEXUAL SEX** was only legalised in 1967.

KINSEY AND THE SEXUAL REVOLUTION

The Kinsey report of 1945 shocked America. Intimate surveys of real people's preferences revealed:

1. 10% of men were homosexual for at least three years of their lives. How then could sexual preference be **UNCHANGING**, fixed and uniform?

2. 26% of married women had extramarital experiences of different sorts.

3. 90% of men masturbated.

4. 50% of men had been unfaithful to their wives.

CHRISTIAN VIEW OF SEX

NATURAL LAW

Aquinas taught that there were three rational ends of sex, arising from the **PRIMARY PRECEPT** of reproduction:

1. To have children.

2. To give **PLEASURE**.

3. To bind husband and wife together.

His view – that sex was for pleasure, was widely condemned, Aquinas wrote "the exceeding pleasure experienced in sex does not destroy the balance of nature as long as it is in harmony with reason". Right reason involves a delicate balance of the three purposes of sex – and avoidance of irrational or animal extremes. So the following sexual sins were forbidden:

1. **Rape**

2. **Casual sex**

3. **Adultery**

4. **Homosexual sex**

5. **Masturbation**

Aquinas' view echoed the erotic celebration of sexual ecstasy in the **SONG OF SONGS** in the Hebrew Bible where sex is a sacred gift and picture of a mystical union, and one of the highest spiritual as well as physical forms of being.

> Behold you are beautiful, my love;
>
> behold you are beautiful;
>
> your eyes are like doves,
>
> Behold you are beautiful my beloved, truly lovely....
>
> Your two breasts are like two fawns,
>
> twins of a gazelle that feed among the lilies...
>
> You have ravished my heart with a glance of your eyes.
>
> (Song of Songs 1:15; 4:2, 5 & 9)

This is one of two parallel strains in the Bible – one positive and one negative, and the positive strain, that sex is to be celebrated, is echoed by Jesus himself, quoting Genesis 2:24, "from the beginning God created them male and female, and for this reason a man shall leave his mother and father and be united with his wife, and the two shall become one flesh. So what God has joined together, let no-one divide" (Mark 10:6-9). See also Paul in Ephesians 5:31.

THE NEGATIVE STRAIN

There is also a negative strain in Christianity which sees sex as dangerous, unclean, and sexual pleasure as sinful.

AUGUSTINE wrote that marriage was the "first fellowship of humankind in this mortal life", and "good not just for producing children, but also because of the natural friendship between the sexes", although primarily "a remedy for weakness, and source of comfort". Ultimately the good of marriage lay in its "goodness, fidelity and unbreakable bond". (13, 17)

Augustine argued against the **PELAGIANS** who saw sexual pleasure as a **NATURAL GOOD**, evil only in excess. Augustine agreed with Paul that since the FALL the body had been subject to death, "our body weighs heavy on our soul" with its sinful desires. Augustine believed that since the fall desire had been tainted by **LUST**. So sexual pleasure in marriage needed to be moderated by reason.

Sexual desire ("the carnal appetite") outside marriage, and sexual activity that results, "is not good, but an evil that comes from original sin". This evil of carnal lust can invade even marriage – so it is **DANGEROUS** and needs to be treated wisely and carefully.

After the **FALL** (Genesis 3) men and women were "naked and ashamed". The man's member is "no longer obedient to a quiet and normal will". Humankind was in danger of running away with lust for each other.

CONCLUSION: Augustine argues that precisely because the body is created good, it can be used wrongly, and this goodness has been deeply stained by the Fall. Sexual desire has to be circumscribed by **MODESTY**, chastity and wisdom.

CATHOLIC TEACHING TODAY

The Roman Catholic Church teaches that sex has two functions – procreative and **UNITIVE** (binding two people together). Procreation is primary. According to Humanae Vitae (1967) these two elements are **INSEPARABLE**.

> "Sexuality becomes fully human when it is integrated into the relationship of one person to the other in lifelong gift of a man to a woman". Catechism 2338

CHASTITY is the virtue of self-mastery (Catechism 2339). It is expressed in friendship towards our neighbour. Sex outside marriage is "gravely contrary to the dignity of persons and of human sexuality which is naturally ordered to the procreation of children". Catechism 2354

HOMOSEXUAL ACTS are "intrinsically disordered". "They are contrary to the natural law. They close the sexual act to the gift of life. Under no circumstances can they be approved". Catechism 2358

ADULTERY is absolutely forbidden by the sixth commandment and Jesus' words.

CONTRACEPTION - in 1951 Pope Pius XII officially permitted the rhythm method, but otherwise Humanae Vitae (1967) upholds the view that anything that breaks the natural relationship between sex and conception is wrong.

EVALUATION OF THE CATHOLIC VIEW

1. Professor Peter Gomes of Harvard University argues that the Bible bans one **CULTURAL** expression of homosexuality – a promiscuous one and "never contemplated a form of homosexuality in which loving and faithful persons sought to live out the implications of the gospel with as much fidelity as any heterosexual believer". The Good Book (1997)

2. The Catholic interpretation of natural law implies that the primary function of sex is reproduction. But suppose the primary purpose is **BONDING**, then the argument that sex is purely for reproduction falls down – we can be Natural Law theorists and disagree about the secondary precepts (which Aquinas always argues are relative).

3. The Catholic **ASSUMPTION** (following Aquinas) is of one human nature. But psychology suggests there are varieties of human nature (heterosexual, homosexual, bisexual) because of genes or environment.

4. The prohibition on **CONTRACEPTION** seems irrational in a world of overpopulation and **STD**s. If **PRESERVATION OF LIFE** conflicts with **REPRODUCTION**, surely preservation of life is the primary primary precept?

SITUATION ETHICS – CHRISTIAN RELATIVISM

Joseph Fletcher sees his own theory as **RELATIVISTIC** (even though it retains one absolute principle, agape love) because any decision is made relative to circumstances.

ABSOLUTE rules must be rejected as authoritarian and unloving.

Biblical prescriptions should be followed as wise **ADVICE** but abandoned in extreme situations if love demands it.

Fletcher argues that many applications of morality are never discussed in the Bible: "Jesus said nothing about birth control, homosexuality, pre-marital intercourse, homosexuality, sex play, petting or courtship". (Fletcher, page 80).

> "It seems impossible to see any sound reason for any of the attempts to legislate morality. It is doubtful whether love's cause is helped by any of the sex laws that try to dictate sexual practices for consenting adults". Fletcher page 80

AGAPE love (unconditional love) is the only norm. The situationist is not a 'what asker', ("what sexual practice is allowed?) but a 'who asker'. It's about **PERSONALISM** – people come first.

EVALUATION OF CHRISTIAN RELATIVISM

1. **AGAPE** is too high a standard for our personal relationships, usually governed by self-interest. Why should I be loving (rather than pleasure-seeking)?

2.

3. The vulnerable (young, homeless, poor) need the protection of laws preventing **ABUSE** and **EXPLOITATION**.

4. We cannot predict **CONSEQUENCES** eg unwanted pregnancies or **STD**s happen to people not expecting them who may honestly believe they love the other person.

HOMOSEXUAL ACTS – A TEST CASE

We have already seen that the Catholic Church condemns homosexual behaviour as intrinsically disordered because of the assumption of one **UNIFORM HUMAN NATURE**. The situationist takes the opposite view; such legalism is unloving and so wrong. Is there a middle way?

In the **ANGLICAN** church there are two gay bishops (in America) and many practising gay priests. **VIRTUE ETHICS** indicates there is a third way of analysing homosexual behaviour. Which **VIRTUES** are present in the relationship? The **EXCESS** of promiscuity is condemned, but faithfulness, care and compassion can apply in any relationship irrespective of orientation. By the same argument the **DEFICIENCY** of abstinence is also a character **VICE**.

The moral issue surrounding homosexuality should therefore be about the promiscuous lifestyle and irresponsible spread of disease (as with heterosexuals). The legalism of natural law or over-emphasis on the code of Leviticus blinds us to the true moral question. What **VALUES** do we need in order to **FLOURISH**?

KANT on SEX

Kant asks us to commit to build the moral world – the **SUMMUM BONUM** or greatest good, by following the rational principle he calls the **CATEGORICAL IMPERATIVE**. This principle has to be applied in all similar circumstances without conditions – it is **ABSOLUTE**. We have to act in such a way that we can imagine a universal law where everyone follows the rule that is generated.

1. Humans have intrinsic **VALUE** as "ends in themselves". We must be given equal dignity and respect as autonomous rational beings.

2. We share an irrational nature of passions and instincts with **ANIMALS** but we can rise above these and order our lives by reason. Human sex will be different from animal urges.

3. **LUST** disturbs reason. By desiring someone simply as an object of pleasure (rather than seeing them as a whole person, with dignity and reason) we dishonour them and violate their special uniqueness as a free person. We sink to the level of animals.

"Sex exposes mankind to the danger of equality with the beasts...by virtue of the nature of sexual desire a person who sexually desires another person objectifies that person..and makes of the loved person an object of appetite. As soon as that appetite is satisfied one casts aside the person as one casts aside a lemon that has been sucked dry". Lectures on Ethics

MARRIAGE is the best expression of our sexuality. The pleasure of sex is acceptable (ie not animal) because two people surrender their dignity to each other and permit each other's bodies to be used for this purpose

– it is a mutual **CONSENSUAL CONTRACT**. Reproduction is not the end of sex, Kant argues, but lifelong surrender to each other in a context of love and respect.

EVALUATION OF KANT

1. Kant appears to separate our **ANIMAL** nature from our **RATIONAL**. This dualism explains why he still sees sex as something belonging to the animal nature. But **FEELINGS** and **REASON** cannot be separated this way, many would argue.

2. Kantian ethics produces **ABSOLUTES** (Categoricals). So the absolute "no sex before marriage" applies here. But in the modern era such absolutes seem to deny the possibility of a **TEMPORARY** committed relationship – or even sex for fun.

3. It's possible to be a Kantian and accept **HOMOSEXUAL MARRIAGE** but not **ADULTERY**.

UTILITARIANISM

What do the utilitarians say about our four issues: contraception, pre-marital sex, adultery and homosexuality? Here we contrast **MILL** (1806-73) and **SINGER** (1946-).

Mill is a **MULTILEVEL** utilitarian who follows a more **ARISTOTELEAN** idea of happiness – eudaimonia or personal and social flourishing. He argues that we need **RULES** to protect justice and **RIGHTS**, which are the cumulative wisdom of society. But when happiness demands it, or a **CONFLICT** of values occurs, we revert to being an **ACT** utilitarian – hence multilevel (Act and Rule) utilitarianism.

Mill agreed that **CONTRACEPTION** was moral as it increased personal and social happiness, through family planning and restrictions on population growth. Today the British Humanist association writes "if contraception results in every child being a wanted child and in better, healthier lives for women, it must be a good thing". Mill was imprisoned in 1832 for distributing "diabolical handbills" advocating contraception.

Mill had found a murdered baby in a park. The practice of exposing unwanted children was widespread. Hospitals for **FOUNDLINGS** such as **CORAM** set up in Bristol in 1741, did little except institutionalise **INFANTICIDE** (child killing). Between 1728 and 1757 33% of babies born in foundling hospitals and workhouses died or were deliberately killed.

On **HOMOSEXUAL** rights Mill follows Bentham in arguing for "utilitarian equality" by which everyone's happiness counts equally. Bentham was the first philosopher to suggest legalised **SODOMY** in an unpublished paper in 1802. Freedom was a key to personal flourishing, and as long as no harm was done to any but consenting adults, it is a private matter how people order their sex lives.

In his essay on **LIBERTY** (1859) Mill argues for **SOCIAL RIGHTS** so we can undertake "experiments in living" that give us protection from the taboos and prejudices of popular culture and "the tyranny of prevailing opinion and feeling". Mill would have approved of **COHABITATION** and pre-marital sex.

EVALUATION OF MILL

Mill was a father of the liberalism we take for granted where difference is tolerated. His brand of utilitarianism balances social justice and individual freedom and pursuit of happiness.

1. Utilitarianism works well looking **BACKWARDS**. The Abortion Act (1967), the Homosexual Reform Act (1967) and the Divorce Reform Act (1969) are all examples of utilitarian legislation.

2. Utilitarian ethics works less well looking forwards. We cannot predict **CONSEQUENCES**. So the **AIDS** epidemic can be seen as a product partly of personal freedom to adopt a promiscuous "unsafe" lifestyle. It is hard to see how a utilitarian can prevent this or even argue it is wrong if freely chosen.

3. Many of the greatest **SOCIAL** reforms have not been inspired by Christian values, Natural Law or Kantian ethics, but by UTILITARIAN considerations of social **WELFARE**. Today relatively few Christian churches accept the complete equality of women.

PREFERENCE UTILITARIANISM

Peter Singer defends the utilitarian line advanced by Mill and argued that with **HOMOSEXUALITY** "If a form of sexual activity brings satisfaction to those who take part in it, and harms no-one, what can be immoral about it?" Peter Singer

On **ADULTERY** preference utilitarians approve of any sexual activity which maximises the preferences of individuals, taking account the preferences of all those affected. So incest, bestiality, or adultery would all be acceptable.

Singer as argues for **CONTRACEPTION** as population growth is one of the most pressing utilitarian issues, we should "help governments make contraception and sterilisation as widespread as possible" (Practical Ethics page 183). But overseas aid should be made conditional on adoption of contraceptives.

KEY QUOTES - SEXUAL ETHICS

1. "The only purpose for which power can be rightfully exercised over any member of a civilised community against his will, is to prevent harm to others. His own good, either physical or moral, is not sufficient warrant". JS Mill

2. "If a form of sexual activity brings satisfaction to those who take part in it, and harms no-one, what can be immoral about it?" Peter Singer

3. "The pleasure derived from the union between the sexes us a pleasure: therefore, leaving aside the evils, which derive from that source here is why the legislator must do whatever is in his power so that the quantity in society is as high as possible". Jeremy Bentham

4. "Sex exposes mankind to the danger of equality with the beasts...by virtue of the nature of sexual desire a person who sexually desires another person objectifies that person..and makes of the loved person an object of appetite. As soon as that appetite is satisfied one casts aside the person as one casts aside a lemon that has been sucked dry ". Kant

5. "It seems impossible to see any sound reason for any of the attempts to legislate morality. It is doubtful whether love's cause is helped by any of the sex laws that try to dictate sexual practices for consenting adults". Joseph Fletcher

Exam Rescue Remedy

1. Build your own scaffolding which represents the logic of the theory. Use a mind map or a summary sheet.

2. Do an analysis of past questions by theme as well as by year (see philosophicalinvestigations.co.uk website).

3. Examine examiners' reports for clues as to how to answer a question well.

4. Use the **DARM** approach suggested in my revision guide. How is goodness derived by this theory? How is the idea of goodness applied? How realistic is this theory – does it fit with your own experience of making moral decisions? Does it answer the question of motivation – why should I be moral?.

5. List relevant technical vocabulary for inclusion in essay (eg synderesis, primary precepts, secondary precepts, eudaimonia).

6. Prepare key quotes from selected key authors, original/ contemporary (eg quotes list from philosophicalinvestigations.co.uk website – even better, produce your own). Learn some.

7. Contrast and then evaluate different views/theories/authors as some questions ask "which theory is best?" So contrast every theory with one other and decide beforehand what you think.

8. Practise writing for 35 minutes. Don't use a computer, unless you do so in the exam.

9. Always answer and discuss the exact question in front of you, never learn a "model answer". Use your own examples (newspapers, films, documentaries, real life).

10. Conclude with your view, justify it (give reasons) especially with "discuss".

Postscript

Peter Baron read Politics, Philosophy and Economics at New College, Oxford and afterwards obtained an MLitt for a research degree in Hermeneutics at Newcastle University. He qualified as an Economics teacher in 1982, and since 2006 has taught ethics at Wells Cathedral School in Somerset.

In 2007 he set up a philosophy and ethics community dedicated to enlarging the teaching of philosophy in schools by applying the theory of multiple intelligences to the analysis of philosophical and ethical problems. So far 200 schools have joined the community and over 9,000 individuals use his website every month.

To join the community please register your interest by filling in your details on the form on the website. We welcome contributions and suggestions so that our community continues to flourish and expand.

www.philosophicalinvestigations.co.uk